# Atheist Spirituality: Beyond Belief

Tony Churchill

Published by Tony Churchill, 2024.

# Atheist Spirituality:
## Beyond Belief

## by Tony Churchill

© 2024

While every precaution has been taken in the preparation of this book, the publisher assumes no responsibility for errors or omissions, or for damages resulting from the use of the information contained herein.

ATHEIST SPIRITUALITY: BEYOND BELIEF

**First edition. April 4, 2024.**

Copyright © 2024 Tony Churchill.

ISBN: 979-8224414031

Written by Tony Churchill.

# EPIGRAPH

"Man is what he believes."
— Anton Chekhov

# DEDICATION

This book is dedicated to all like-minded seekers—those who, like me, have embarked on a quest to understand the profound mysteries of existence without relying on the supernatural. It's for those who find awe in the natural world, meaning in ethical living and purpose in connecting with others.

To those who dare to question, to explore and to seek the extraordinary within the ordinary, this book is for you. May it inspire you to continue on your path of wonder, compassion and intellectual curiosity.

With heartfelt dedication,
Tony Churchill

# PROLOGUE

Exploring Atheist Spirituality

I'm excited to welcome you to this unique journey into the world of atheist spirituality. Now, you might be wondering, "Atheism and spirituality? Aren't they polar opposites?" Well, that's the intriguing thing about this topic—it's not as black and white as it might seem.

In these pages, we're going to embark on an exploration of a worldview that doesn't rely on the supernatural yet is brimming with depth, meaning and connection to the world around us. It's a perspective that celebrates life, ethics, reason and our place in the grand tapestry of existence.

But first, let me be clear about something. This book isn't about convincing you to become an atheist or to embrace any particular set of beliefs. Nope, it's about understanding, appreciating and delving into a worldview that is sometimes overlooked in discussions of spirituality.

Atheist spirituality isn't about rituals or dogma. It's about finding wonder in the natural world, deriving meaning from ethical living and fostering connections with our fellow human beings. It's about curiosity, skepticism and the celebration of life itself.

Throughout these chapters, we'll explore the various facets of this intriguing worldview. We'll dive into topics like ethics, mindfulness, community, intellectual curiosity and the pursuit of knowledge—all from an atheist perspective.

So whether you're an atheist looking to explore your own spirituality or simply curious about the diverse beliefs that shape our world, this book is for you. Let's embark on this journey together and discover the rich and meaningful world of atheist spirituality.

Ready? Let's dive in!

# Chapter 1: Defining Atheist Spirituality

I'm here to kick off this adventure into the world of atheist spirituality. Now, I know what some of you might be thinking. "Atheism and spirituality? Aren't those two completely opposing things?" Well, I'm here to tell you that they don't have to be.

Let's start by breaking it down. Atheism, in a nutshell, is the belief that there's no supernatural, all-powerful being or beings pulling the strings of the universe. It's a perspective that says, "Hey, we're on our own here and that's okay." It's often associated with science, reason and a healthy dose of skepticism.

Spirituality, on the other hand, typically conjures up images of meditation, prayer and connecting with something greater than ourselves. It's often seen as a deeply personal and, well, *spiritual* experience.

So how do we combine these seemingly contradictory ideas into something meaningful? That's the question I aim to explore in this book.

For me, atheism isn't about rejecting the search for meaning or dismissing the wonders of the world. It's about embracing those things in a way that's grounded in reason and the here-and-now. It's about finding awe in the grandeur of the universe, the complexity of life and the beauty of human connection, all without invoking the supernatural.

In these pages, we're going to delve into what it means to live a life rich in atheist spirituality. We'll talk about finding meaning in a world without gods, the power of mindfulness and the ethics that guide us without divine commandments.

But it's not just about philosophy and ideas; it's about practicality, too. We'll explore atheist rituals, meditation practices and ways to cultivate a sense of wonder in our daily lives. We'll also discuss how atheism can intersect with issues like social justice and environmentalism because, hey, we're not living in a vacuum.

So whether you're a seasoned atheist, a curious skeptic, or just someone looking for a different perspective on spirituality, stick around. We're embarking on a journey of discovery together and who knows, you might find a whole new way to see the world. Thanks for joining me and let's get started!

# Chapter 2: The Origins of Atheism

Atheism, like any belief system, didn't just pop out of thin air. It has a history and understanding where it comes from can shed light on why people like us embrace it.

If we rewind the clock back through the annals of time, we'll find that atheistic or non-theistic ideas have been around for a long, long while. In ancient Greece, for example, thinkers like Epicurus and Democritus were questioning the existence of gods as far back as the 5th century BCE.

However, atheism often took a backseat to the prevailing religious beliefs of the day. In many ancient societies, it wasn't exactly safe to declare your disbelief in the local gods. That might earn you a one-way ticket to exile or worse.

Fast forward a bit to the Enlightenment period in Europe during the 17th and 18th centuries. This was a game-changer. Thinkers like Voltaire and David Hume started pushing back against religious dogma and championing reason and skepticism. The idea that humans could use their minds to understand the world without divine intervention gained traction.

The 19th century saw the rise of atheism as a more organized movement. Figures like Charles Darwin shook the foundations of religious creationism with his theory of evolution. And as science continued to advance, many found it increasingly difficult to reconcile religious texts with empirical evidence.

The 20th century brought us even more prominent atheist voices, from philosophers like Bertrand Russell to scientists like Carl Sagan. Atheism wasn't just a philosophical position; it was becoming a social and cultural force, especially in more secularized societies.

Now, in the 21st century, atheism is more visible and accepted than ever before. The internet has allowed atheists to connect, share ideas and find like-minded communities in ways that were unimaginable just a few decades ago.

So when we talk about the origins of atheism, it's not just about dusty old books and ancient philosophers. It's a story of human curiosity, the pursuit of knowledge and the evolution of thought. And it's a story that continues to unfold as more and more people explore the idea that we can find meaning and purpose in life without appealing to the divine.

# Chapter 3: The Evolution of Spirituality

You know, spirituality isn't just about incense, meditation cushions and chanting "Om" in a darkened room. It's a dynamic and evolving concept that has taken on many forms throughout human history. So let's dive into the ever-changing landscape of spirituality.

**Ancient Roots:** Way back in the day, our ancestors were already getting spiritual. They looked to nature, the stars and the cycles of life for meaning. Shamanistic practices, animism and ancestor worship were some of the earliest forms of spirituality. These were attempts to connect with something beyond the everyday, to tap into a deeper, more mysterious realm.

**The Birth of Organized Religion:** As societies grew more complex, so did spirituality. Organized religions like Christianity, Islam, Buddhism and Hinduism emerged. These brought structured beliefs, rituals and moral codes. They offered a sense of community and answers to the big questions, but they also came with dogma and sometimes division.

**Mysticism and Enlightenment:** Alongside organized religions, mystics and philosophers started exploring the mystical side of spirituality. Think of folks like Rumi, Meister Eckhart and the Zen masters. They sought direct experiences of the divine, often outside the confines of religious institutions. Meanwhile, the Enlightenment in the 18th century emphasized reason over faith, sparking a more secular form of spirituality.

**New Age and Beyond:** The 20th century saw a resurgence of interest in spirituality beyond traditional religious boundaries. The New Age movement brought concepts like holistic healing, meditation and crystal energy into the mainstream. People began to explore spirituality as a deeply personal journey, often outside of organized religion.

**Science and Spirituality:** Interestingly, as our scientific understanding of the universe expanded, it didn't necessarily push spirituality to the sidelines. In fact, it sometimes gave it a new context. Figures like Carl Sagan and Neil deGrasse Tyson showed that you could find wonder and awe in the natural world without invoking the supernatural.

**Contemporary Spirituality:** Today, spirituality is more diverse than ever. Some find it in nature, others in art and some in secular practices like mindfulness and yoga. It's about seeking purpose, connection and a sense of transcendence in a world where traditional religious structures are no longer the sole authority.

So what does all this mean for atheist spirituality? Well, it means that we're part of a long and ever-evolving story. We're redefining what it means to be spiritual in a world that's increasingly secular. We're finding awe and wonder in the cosmos, in human connection and in the simple act of being alive. And we're doing it in a way that's true to our rational, skeptical and deeply human selves.

# Chapter 4: Navigating Life's Meaning Without a Deity

Alright, so here's the big question: if you disbelieve in a higher power, where do you find meaning in life? It's a puzzle that atheists often grapple with, but fear not, we're diving into it headfirst.

**The Search for Purpose:** Let's start with the idea of purpose. For many people, religion provides a ready-made answer. You're here to serve God, follow his commandments and eventually, earn a spot in paradise. But for atheists, it's a bit different. We believe that life's purpose isn't handed down from on high; it's something we have to discover for ourselves.

**Humanism and Ethics:** One of the cornerstones of atheist spirituality is humanism. It's a philosophy that places humans, their welfare and their values at the center of things. Humanists believe in doing good for the sake of humanity, not because they're trying to score points with a deity. So finding meaning in helping others, in contributing to the greater good, is a big part of our game plan.

**Personal Fulfillment:** Atheists often find meaning in personal fulfillment and self-actualization. This might mean pursuing your passions, nurturing your talents, or simply enjoying the pleasures of life. We see this life as the only one we've got, so making the most of it becomes a pretty important mission.

**Connection and Relationships:** Human connection is another major source of meaning. Whether it's through family, friends, or broader communities, relationships give our lives depth and purpose. Caring for others and being cared for in return can be profoundly meaningful experiences.

**The Pursuit of Knowledge:** Many atheists are avid seekers of knowledge. We find meaning in the pursuit of truth and understanding, whether that's through science, philosophy, or just good old-fashioned curiosity. The idea that we can uncover the mysteries of the universe through our own efforts can be incredibly inspiring.

**Embracing the Present:** Atheist spirituality often emphasizes the importance of living in the moment. Since we disbelieve in an afterlife, the here and now takes on extra significance. Finding meaning in everyday experiences, in the beauty of the natural world, or even in a great book or film becomes a way of celebrating life.

**Creating Your Own Meaning:** Ultimately, atheist spirituality is about crafting your own meaning. It's a highly individualistic approach. You get to decide what matters most to you, what gives your life purpose and what makes it all worth it.

So there you have it. Life's meaning without a deity is a journey of self-discovery, human connection, personal fulfillment and the pursuit of knowledge. It's about celebrating the beauty and complexity of this world, all on our terms. It might not come with a ready-made script, but that's precisely what makes it so exciting and uniquely yours.

# Chapter 5: Embracing Humanism

Alright, we've talked about finding meaning in life without the supernatural, but what's this humanism thing all about and why is it such a big deal for atheists? Let's break it down.

**The Heart of Humanism:** At its core, humanism is a philosophy that places humans at the forefront. It's not about worshiping a deity or subscribing to a particular dogma. Instead, it's a celebration of human potential, ethics and values.

**Reason and Rationality:** Humanism values reason and rationality as the best tools we have for understanding the world. It encourages critical thinking, evidence-based decision-making and a commitment to the scientific method. In other words, it's all about using our brains to figure things out.

**Ethics Without Divine Commandments:** One of the key aspects of humanism is its approach to ethics. Unlike religious systems that derive morality from divine commandments, humanism sees ethics as a product of human reason, empathy and social cooperation. We don't need a god telling us what's right and wrong; we can figure it out ourselves.

**Empathy and Compassion:** Humanism places a strong emphasis on empathy and compassion. It's about recognizing the inherent dignity and worth of every individual and striving for the well-being of all. The Golden Rule — treating others as you'd like to be treated — is a fundamental principle.

**Secularism and Separation of Church and State:** Humanism advocates for the separation of church and state. It believes that governments should be secular, treating all citizens equally, regardless of their religious beliefs (or choice for none). This ensures that no one group's beliefs are imposed on others.

**Social Justice and Equality:** Humanists often engage in social justice activism. This means working to address inequalities and fighting for the rights of marginalized groups. Humanism isn't just about personal fulfillment; it's about making the world a better place for everyone.

**Personal Fulfillment:** While humanism places a strong emphasis on the collective good, it also values personal fulfillment. Pursuing your passions, achieving your potential and finding happiness are all seen as valuable aspects of a fulfilling life.

**The Joy of Discovery:** Humanists find joy in the pursuit of knowledge and understanding. They see the world as a place of wonder, where each discovery brings us closer to unraveling its mysteries. Learning, exploring and expanding our horizons are all part of the humanist ethos.

**Atheism and Humanism:** Many atheists identify as humanists because of the shared emphasis on reason, ethics and the human experience. However, it's important to note that not all atheists are humanists and not all humanists are atheists. Humanism is a broader philosophy that can be embraced by people with various belief systems.

So when you hear someone talk about humanism, know that it's not just a buzzword. It's a philosophy that champions the power of human reason, compassion and ethical living. It's about making the world a better place, not because a deity commands it, but because we believe it's the right thing to do.

# Chapter 6: Finding Wonder in the Natural World

Ever taken a moment to just stare up at the night sky and feel that sense of awe and wonder? Or perhaps you've hiked through a dense forest, hearing the rustle of leaves underfoot and feeling the life all around you. These are the moments when atheists often find a deep connection with the natural world.

**The Grandeur of the Universe:** You don't need to believe in a higher power to be absolutely amazed by the universe. The vastness of space, the billions of galaxies and the intricate dance of celestial bodies can leave you in awe. Science has given us the tools to understand some of these cosmic wonders and it's a journey that never gets old.

**The Complexity of Life:** Life on Earth is nothing short of astonishing. The incredible diversity of species, from the tiniest microorganisms to the largest mammals, is a testament to the beauty of evolution. Exploring the intricacies of ecosystems and the interconnectedness of all living things can be a profoundly spiritual experience for atheists.

**The Power of Science:** Atheists often turn to science as a source of wonder. It's not just about facts and figures; it's about the process of discovery itself. The scientific method, with its emphasis on observation, experimentation and evidence, opens up a world of understanding. It's a way to uncover the mysteries of the universe, step by step.

**Nature as a Teacher:** Many atheists see nature as a wise teacher. It's a place to learn about balance, adaptation and resilience. The natural world can inspire us to find our own equilibrium and face life's challenges with strength and grace.

**Environmental Stewardship:** For atheists, a sense of wonder often leads to a commitment to environmental stewardship. When you're in awe of the natural world, you want to protect it. Many atheists engage in environmental activism and conservation efforts because they see the value of preserving the planet for future generations.

**Art and Expression:** Nature often serves as a wellspring of inspiration for artists. Whether it's a painter capturing the play of light on a mountain or a musician composing a symphony inspired by the ocean, the natural world has a way of sparking creativity and deep emotional expression.

**Finding Spirituality in Everyday Moments:** Atheist spirituality isn't just about grand vistas; it's about finding wonder in everyday life. A perfectly brewed cup of coffee, the laughter of a child, or the warmth of a hug can all be moments of deep connection and spirituality for atheists.

So while atheists might not attribute the wonders of the world to a deity, they certainly find plenty to be amazed by. Whether it's the cosmos, the beauty of life, or the simple pleasures of existence, atheists revel in the awe-inspiring grandeur of the natural world. It's a source of spirituality that's right here, all around us, waiting to be discovered.

# Chapter 7: The Power of Mindfulness

Picture this: You're sitting in a quiet room, eyes closed, focusing on your breath. Your mind is no longer racing with thoughts of the past or worries about the future. You're fully present in the here and now. That, my friends, is the power of mindfulness.

**What is Mindfulness?:** Mindfulness is a practice that involves paying deliberate attention to the present moment without judgment. It's about being fully aware of your thoughts, feelings, bodily sensations and the world around you. It's like hitting the pause button on life and just being.

**The Roots of Mindfulness:** While mindfulness has gained popularity in recent years, it's far from a new concept. It has deep roots in Buddhist meditation practices, where it's known as "sati." Buddhists have been practicing mindfulness for over 2,500 years as a means to achieve insight, wisdom and inner peace.

**The Mind-Body Connection:** Mindfulness emphasizes the mind-body connection. It's about tuning in to the sensations in your body and the thoughts in your mind. This awareness can lead to a better understanding of your emotional and physical well-being.

**Stress Reduction:** One of the most well-documented benefits of mindfulness is its ability to reduce stress. By staying present and letting go of worries about the past and future, you can lower your stress levels and experience greater calm.

**Improved Mental Health:** Mindfulness has been shown to have positive effects on mental health. It can help with anxiety, depression and even post-traumatic stress disorder (PTSD). By observing your thoughts without judgment, you can gain perspective on your mental state.

**Enhanced Focus and Concentration:** Practicing mindfulness can sharpen your focus and concentration. In a world filled with distractions, this is a valuable skill. It can improve your performance at work or in any task that requires your full attention.

Mindfulness often involves cultivating gratitude. When you're fully present, you can appreciate the small joys of life—the taste of your favorite food, the warmth of the sun on your skin, or the sound of laughter. Gratitude can lead to a more positive outlook on life.

**Compassion and Empathy:** Mindfulness can also enhance compassion and empathy. By tuning in to your own feelings and experiences, you become more attuned to the emotions of others. This can improve your relationships and make you a more compassionate person.

**Mindfulness and Atheist Spirituality:** For atheists, mindfulness is a valuable tool for grounding spirituality in the present moment. It doesn't require belief in the supernatural. Instead, it's about connecting with the here and now, finding meaning in the present and embracing the richness of everyday life.

**Getting Started with Mindfulness:** If you're interested in mindfulness, you don't need any special equipment or guru. You can start with simple practices like mindful breathing or body scanning. There are also many apps and resources available to guide you on your mindfulness journey.

So whether you're seeking stress relief, improved mental health, or a deeper connection with the world around you, mindfulness is a powerful practice that can help. It's a way to experience spirituality in the present moment and it's available to anyone willing to give it a try.

# Chapter 8: Morality and Ethics in an Atheist Framework

Morality and ethics—these are topics that often come up in discussions about atheism. Some folks wonder, "If you disbelieve in God, where do you get your moral compass?" Well, let's dive into the fascinating world of ethics in an atheist framework.

**No Divine Rulebook:** Atheists don't look to a divine rulebook for their morals. Instead, they draw their ethical principles from various sources and these sources can vary from person to person. Here are a few common ones:

**Humanism:** Humanism, as we discussed earlier, is a big deal for many atheists. It places a strong emphasis on human values, well-being and dignity. Humanists believe that ethical decisions should be based on reason, empathy and the greater good of humanity.

**Social and Cultural Values:** Much of our ethical framework is shaped by the society and culture we live in. Laws, norms and customs all play a role in determining what's considered right and wrong. These values are often based on shared human experiences and evolving social dynamics.

**Empathy and Compassion:** Many atheists emphasize empathy and compassion as key moral principles. The ability to understand and share the feelings of others can guide ethical decision-making. After all, if you wouldn't want something done to you, why do it to someone else?

**Rational Ethics:** Some atheists follow ethical systems rooted in reason and logic. Philosophers like Immanuel Kant and John Stuart Mill developed ethical theories that don't rely on religious beliefs. Kant's categorical imperative, for example, encourages treating others as ends in themselves, not as means to an end.

**Consequences Matter:** For many atheists, the consequences of actions play a crucial role in ethical considerations. The ethical theory of consequentialism argues that the rightness or wrongness of an action is determined by its outcomes. This perspective emphasizes the importance of minimizing harm and maximizing well-being.

**Secular Organizations:** Some atheists turn to secular organizations and communities for ethical guidance. These groups often promote values like secular humanism, equality and social justice. They provide a supportive network for individuals seeking to live ethically without religious beliefs.

**Personal Reflection:** Atheists often engage in personal reflection and critical thinking when making ethical decisions. They consider the potential impact of their actions on themselves and others, weighing the ethical implications of their choices.

**Ethical Challenges:** Just like religious individuals, atheists face ethical challenges in their lives. They grapple with questions of honesty, integrity, fairness and compassion. The absence of a religious authority doesn't mean a lack of ethical dilemmas; it simply means a different approach to resolving them.

**A Dynamic Journey:** Ethical decision-making is a dynamic journey for atheists. It involves ongoing exploration, discussion and refinement of one's moral compass. Atheists recognize that ethics isn't a fixed set of rules but a process of thoughtful consideration and growth.

In the end, atheism doesn't leave a moral vacuum. Atheists are just as concerned with living ethical and meaningful lives as anyone else. They draw from a rich tapestry of humanistic values, cultural norms and rational thought to navigate the complexities of right and wrong. It's a journey that reflects the diversity and depth of human ethics and it's anything but morally empty.

# Chapter 9: The Role of Compassion

Compassion—it's a word often associated with religion and spirituality, but it's just as vital in the world of atheism. Let's talk about how atheists view and practice compassion in their lives.

**Empathy and Understanding:** Compassion begins with empathy. It's about truly understanding the feelings and perspectives of others. For atheists, empathy is a cornerstone of ethical behavior. It's not about divine commandments but about recognizing the shared human experience.

**No Divine Reward:** Unlike some religious beliefs where compassion is seen as a ticket to heaven or a way to earn divine favor, atheists typically don't expect any supernatural rewards for being compassionate. For them, compassion is its own reward—it's about making the world a better place, here and now.

**The Golden Rule:** Many atheists embrace the Golden Rule, which is found in various forms across different cultures and religions. It's the idea of treating others as you would like to be treated. It's a simple yet profound principle that guides ethical behavior.

**Secular Humanism:** Secular humanism, a philosophy embraced by many atheists, places a strong emphasis on compassion and ethical living. It's about working to improve the well-being of all humans and promoting social justice and equality.

**Social Activism:** Compassion often drives atheists to engage in social activism. They advocate for the rights of marginalized groups, fight against discrimination and work to address social inequalities. Compassion fuels their commitment to making the world a more just and inclusive place.

**Volunteerism:** Many atheists are active volunteers. They donate their time and resources to various causes, from helping the homeless to supporting environmental initiatives. Compassion motivates them to take action and make a positive impact on their communities.

**Supportive Communities:** Atheist communities often provide support and compassion to their members. They offer a sense of belonging and a network of people who share similar values. This sense of community can be a source of strength and compassion in itself.

**Facing Challenges:** Compassion doesn't mean avoiding difficult conversations or shying away from challenging issues. Atheists recognize that addressing issues like inequality, discrimination and social injustice requires empathy and a commitment to change.

**Compassion and Self-Care:** It's important to note that compassion isn't just directed outward. Self-compassion is also crucial. Atheists understand the importance of taking care of themselves both mentally and physically so they can continue to be compassionate toward others.

**A Shared Humanity:** At its core, compassion for atheists is about recognizing our shared humanity. It's about understanding that we're all in this together, regardless of our religious or non-religious beliefs. It's a reminder that kindness and empathy are universal values that transcend religious boundaries.

In the world of atheism, compassion isn't limited to the realm of the divine. It's a driving force that motivates individuals and communities to make a positive impact on the world. It's a reminder that, regardless of our beliefs or non-beliefs, compassion is a fundamental part of what it means to be human.

# Chapter 10: Cultivating Gratitude

Gratitude, that warm feeling of thankfulness, is something atheists embrace just as much as anyone else. It's a powerful emotion that can enhance our lives in numerous ways. Let's explore how atheists cultivate gratitude in their lives.

**Acknowledging Life's Blessings:** Gratitude begins with acknowledging the positive aspects of life. For atheists, this often means recognizing the simple but profound blessings that come with being alive—health, relationships, moments of joy and the beauty of the world around us.

**Mindfulness and Gratitude:** Mindfulness, a practice we've discussed before, plays a big role in cultivating gratitude. By being fully present in the moment, atheists can more easily notice and appreciate the things they might otherwise take for granted.

**Embracing the Present:** Gratitude often involves embracing the present moment. Atheists understand that life is finite and there's no guarantee of an afterlife. This perspective can lead to a deep appreciation for the here and now.

**Finding Beauty in Everyday Life:** Gratitude doesn't always require grand gestures or life-changing events. It can be found in the small, everyday moments—the smell of freshly baked bread, the sound of laughter, or a kind word from a friend. Atheists value these moments of beauty and take time to savor them.

**Connection and Relationships:** Gratitude extends to the people in our lives. Atheists value the connections they have with family, friends and the broader community. Expressing gratitude to loved ones and fostering those relationships is an important part of their lives.

**Acts of Kindness:** Many atheists engage in acts of kindness as a way of expressing gratitude. They understand that by helping others, they can make a positive impact on the world and, in turn, feel grateful for the opportunity to do so.

**Gratitude in Adversity:** Gratitude isn't limited to good times. Atheists also practice gratitude in times of adversity. It might mean finding lessons in difficult experiences or appreciating the strength and resilience that challenges can bring.

**Cultivating a Positive Outlook:** Gratitude can foster a more positive outlook on life. It shifts the focus from what's lacking to what's present. This positive perspective can lead to greater overall well-being and happiness.

**Journaling and Reflection:** Some atheists keep gratitude journals, where they write down things they're thankful for each day. This practice helps them stay attuned to the positive aspects of life and reinforces feelings of gratitude.

**Celebrating Achievements:** Gratitude often involves celebrating personal achievements and milestones. Atheists take pride in their accomplishments, whether they're big or small and use them as reminders of their capabilities.

In the world of atheism, gratitude isn't about thanking a higher power. It's about appreciating the richness of life, finding joy in everyday moments and recognizing the value of human connection. It's a reminder that, regardless of our beliefs, gratitude is a universal language of appreciation and thankfulness.

# Chapter 11: Rituals and Traditions for Atheists

When people hear the word "ritual," they often think of religious ceremonies or mystical practices. But did you know that atheists have their own meaningful rituals and traditions? Let's explore how atheists create rituals that align with their beliefs and values.

**Marking Milestones:** Just like in many religious traditions, atheists often celebrate life's milestones. Birthdays, weddings and graduations are moments of joy and achievement that atheists commemorate with gatherings of friends and family.

**Secular Celebrations:** Many atheists embrace secular celebrations and holidays. These might include Christmas without the religious aspects, focusing instead on the joy of giving and spending time with loved ones. Easter might involve an egg hunt and a delicious meal, minus the resurrection story.

**Solstices and Equinoxes:** Some atheists draw inspiration from the changing seasons. They celebrate the solstices and equinoxes, marking the transitions between winter and spring, summer and fall. These celebrations often reflect a connection with nature and the cycles of life.

**Sunday Assemblies:** Sunday Assemblies are secular gatherings that mimic the format of religious services but without the religious content. They often include music, inspirational talks and a sense of community. They provide atheists with a space for reflection and connection.

**Memorial Services:** Atheists hold memorial services to honor the lives of loved ones who have passed away. These services can be deeply personal and focus on celebrating the person's life and the impact they had on others.

**Ethical Ceremonies:** Some atheists create ethical ceremonies to mark important life events. For example, a commitment ceremony might be held to celebrate a couple's commitment to each other without the religious connotations of a wedding.

**Secular Weddings:** Many atheists opt for secular wedding ceremonies that emphasize their love and commitment to each other without invoking religious rituals or beliefs. These ceremonies often focus on personal vows and the support of friends and family.

**Coming of Age Celebrations:** Atheists may celebrate coming of age in a secular way. These ceremonies recognize a young person's transition to adulthood and often involve reflection on values and responsibilities.

**Naming Ceremonies:** Instead of religious baptisms, some atheists hold naming ceremonies to welcome a new child into the family and community. These ceremonies can be a way of expressing love and commitment to the child's well-being.

**Science and Reason Celebrations:** For some atheists, science and reason are central to their identity. They might celebrate the achievements of science and human reason with events or gatherings focused on promoting knowledge and critical thinking.

**Personal Rituals:** Atheists also engage in personal rituals that are meaningful to them. These might include meditation or simply taking time for reflection and gratitude.

It's important to note that rituals and traditions for atheists are diverse and highly individualized. They're often designed to align with secular values, emphasize human connections and provide opportunities for personal growth and reflection. While they may not involve prayers or religious symbolism, these rituals hold deep meaning and significance in the lives of atheists.

# Chapter 12: Meditation and Atheist Practice

Meditation, often associated with Eastern religions and spirituality, might not seem like a natural fit for atheists. However, meditation has found a welcoming home among many atheists as a valuable practice for mental and emotional well-being. Let's delve into how meditation fits into the lives of atheists.

**Stress Reduction:** Meditation, including mindfulness, is renowned for its stress-reducing benefits. In our fast-paced, often chaotic world, atheists turn to meditation to find moments of calm and peace. It's a tool for managing the stresses of everyday life.

**Emotional Regulation:** Meditation helps atheists regulate their emotions. By becoming more aware of their thoughts and feelings, they can respond to situations with greater clarity and emotional resilience. It's about taking control of one's reactions.

**Fostering Compassion:** Meditation can also foster compassion and empathy. Some meditation practices focus on generating feelings of love and compassion toward oneself and others. For atheists, this aligns with their humanistic values of empathy and understanding.

**Personal Growth:** Many atheists see meditation as a path to personal growth and self-improvement. It's a way to explore the inner workings of the mind, develop greater self-awareness and work on becoming the best version of oneself.

**Enhancing Focus and Concentration:** Atheists often turn to meditation to enhance their focus and concentration. In a world filled with distractions, the ability to stay present and attentive is a valuable skill for work, learning and daily tasks.

**Atheist Spirituality:** Meditation can be part of an atheist's spiritual practice. While it doesn't involve prayer or devotion to a deity, it can provide a sense of connection to the universe, the natural world, or the broader human experience.

**Atheist Communities and Meditation:** Some atheist communities incorporate meditation into their gatherings as a way of promoting mental and emotional well-being among members. It's a practice that can foster a sense of community and support.

**Personal Meditation Practices:** Atheists also engage in personal meditation practices. These can be as simple as taking a few moments each day to sit quietly and focus on the breath or engaging in more structured meditation sessions.

In essence, meditation for atheists is about enhancing mental and emotional well-being, developing self-awareness and finding moments of calm and clarity in the midst of life's challenges. It's a practice that aligns with atheist values of reason, compassion and personal growth, offering a unique path to spirituality without the need for belief in the supernatural.

# Chapter 13: Atheism and Transcendence

Transcendence, the idea of going beyond ordinary limits or experiencing something beyond the everyday, might not be the first thing that comes to mind when you think of atheism. But for some atheists, moments of transcendence do exist and they can be deeply meaningful.

**Naturalistic Transcendence:** Atheists who experience moments of transcendence often describe them in naturalistic terms. These might be moments of awe and wonder inspired by the beauty of nature, the vastness of the cosmos, or the complexity of life on Earth.

**Science and Understanding:** For many atheists, transcendence can be found in the pursuit of scientific knowledge and understanding. The feeling of unlocking a new piece of the universe's mysteries or grasping a profound scientific concept can be a transcendent experience.

**Art and Creativity:** Atheists often find transcendence in art and creativity. Whether it's through creating art themselves or appreciating the work of others, these moments of beauty and inspiration can transport them beyond the ordinary.

**Connection with Humanity:** Transcendence can also be about feeling deeply connected to humanity. Acts of kindness, moments of empathy and a sense of oneness with the broader human experience can evoke a feeling of transcending individual boundaries.

**Music and Emotion:** Music has the power to stir deep emotions and evoke a sense of transcendence. For atheists, a moving piece of music can transport them to a different emotional and psychological state, transcending the mundane.

**Transcendence in the Everyday:** Atheists often find moments of transcendence in the everyday experiences of life. It might be the taste of a delicious meal, the laughter of a loved one, or the warmth of the sun on their skin. These simple pleasures can evoke a sense of going beyond the ordinary.

**Connection with the Universe:** Atheists sometimes describe a feeling of connection with the universe itself. It's not a connection to a deity but a sense of being part of the grand tapestry of existence, a tiny piece of the cosmos.

**Secular Spirituality:** Transcendence is often a component of secular spirituality for atheists. It's about finding meaning and a sense of wonder in the natural world, the human experience and the pursuit of knowledge.

**No Need for the Supernatural:** Importantly, these moments of transcendence don't require belief in the supernatural. For atheists, they are natural, deeply human experiences that can be deeply fulfilling and meaningful.

In the world of atheism, transcendence isn't about reaching out to a higher power. It's about reaching in, exploring the depths of the human experience and finding moments of awe, wonder and connection in the here and now. It's a reminder that the capacity for transcendent experiences is a fundamental part of being human, regardless of one's religious or non-religious beliefs.

# Chapter 14: Atheist Views on Death and Afterlife

Death, the great unknown, has fascinated and perplexed humanity for millennia. For atheists, the perspective on death and the afterlife is distinct from religious beliefs. Let's delve into how atheists view these profound and often existential questions.

**No Belief in an Afterlife:** The fundamental difference between atheistic and many religious worldviews is the disbelief in an afterlife. Atheists generally disbelieve in the existence of a soul or an eternal self that continues to exist after death.

**Finality of Death:** Atheists see death as the end of conscious existence. When a person dies, their thoughts, memories and consciousness cease to exist. It's a perspective that emphasizes the preciousness of life in the here and now.

**Facing Mortality:** For atheists, accepting the finality of death means facing the reality of mortality head-on. Instead of seeking comfort in the promise of an afterlife, they often focus on making the most of the time they have and leaving a positive legacy.

**Importance of Legacy:** Many atheists place great importance on the legacy they leave behind. This legacy might be in the form of their contributions to society, the impact they've had on others, or the memories they've created with loved ones.

**Comfort in Naturalism:** Atheists find comfort in natural explanations for death. They see death as a natural part of the life cycle, with no need for supernatural or religious explanations. This perspective aligns with their emphasis on reason and evidence.

**Grief and Coping:** Like everyone else, atheists experience grief when a loved one dies. They cope with loss through various means, often relying on the support of friends and family, therapy, or secular grief support groups.

**Moral and Ethical Focus:** Knowing that life is finite often leads atheists to focus on ethical living and making a positive impact on the world. The absence of an afterlife reinforces the importance of treating others with kindness and leaving the world a better place.

**Living in the Present:** The awareness of life's impermanence encourages atheists to live in the present moment. It's a reminder to cherish the time they have with loved ones, pursue their passions and find meaning in the here and now.

**Existential Reflection:** The absence of an afterlife can lead atheists to engage in existential reflection. They grapple with questions of meaning, purpose and the nature of existence. These reflections often lead to a deep appreciation for the beauty and complexity of life.

**Secular Funerals and Memorials:** Many atheists choose to have secular funerals or memorials when they or their loved ones pass away. These ceremonies often focus on celebrating the person's life and the impact they had on others, rather than religious rituals or beliefs.

In essence, for atheists, death is not a gateway to an afterlife, but a natural and inevitable part of the human experience. It's a perspective that encourages them to make the most of their time on Earth, find meaning in their actions and embrace the preciousness of life in the absence of supernatural beliefs about what comes next.

# Chapter 15: Philosophy and Atheist Spirituality

Atheism often intersects with philosophy in intriguing ways, especially when it comes to spirituality. Let's explore how philosophy shapes atheist spirituality and provides a foundation for their beliefs and values.

**Secular Humanism:** Many atheists align with the philosophy of secular humanism. This worldview places humans at the center, emphasizing reason, ethics and compassion. It serves as a moral and philosophical framework for atheist spirituality.

**Ethical Philosophy:** Atheists often draw on ethical philosophy to guide their moral compass. Philosophical theories like utilitarianism, deontology and virtue ethics offer secular approaches to understanding right and wrong.

**Existentialism:** Existentialist philosophy, with its exploration of individual existence and freedom, resonates with some atheists. It invites introspection and reflection on the nature of human existence and the search for meaning.

**Naturalism:** Naturalism is a philosophical viewpoint that asserts that everything in the universe is a result of natural processes, without the need for supernatural explanations. It underpins the atheist perspective on the natural world and the absence of a divine creator.

**Epistemology:** Atheists often engage with epistemology, the study of knowledge and belief. They emphasize the importance of evidence, reason and critical thinking in forming beliefs, including those related to spirituality or the choice for none.

**Skepticism:** Skepticism is a philosophical stance that encourages doubt and questioning. Atheists often adopt a skeptical approach when examining religious claims and supernatural beliefs. They seek empirical evidence and rational arguments to support their views.

**Atheist Existentialism:** Some atheists embrace an existentialist worldview that centers on individual freedom and choice in the absence of divine guidance. This philosophy encourages personal responsibility for shaping one's life.

**Secular Ethics:** Atheists engage in discussions about secular ethics, exploring how to live meaningful and ethical lives without relying on religious guidelines. These discussions often involve philosophical inquiry into human values and well-being.

**Philosophical Inquiry:** Atheist spirituality includes philosophical inquiry into the nature of existence, consciousness and the universe. These deep questions invite atheists to explore their place in the cosmos.

**Awe and Wonder:** While atheists may not attribute the wonders of the world to a deity, they find awe and wonder in the natural world and the mysteries of the universe. This sense of wonder serves as a source of atheist spirituality.

**Interconnectedness:** Some atheists draw from philosophical ideas of interconnectedness to foster a sense of unity with all living beings and the environment. This interconnectedness serves as a foundation for their spiritual experiences.

**Ethical and Existential Dilemmas:** Philosophy provides atheists with tools to navigate ethical and existential dilemmas. They engage in critical thinking and moral reflection to address life's challenges and make informed decisions.

In the realm of atheist spirituality, philosophy plays a vital role in shaping beliefs, values and the pursuit of meaning. It provides a rational and ethical foundation for understanding the world, living ethically and finding spirituality in the absence of religious beliefs.

# Chapter 16: Atheist Approaches to Happiness

Happiness, that elusive yet cherished state of well-being, is a pursuit that atheists, like people of all beliefs, seek to understand and achieve. Let's explore how atheists approach happiness and what principles guide their pursuit of a fulfilling life.

**Secular Values:** Many atheists align with secular values that emphasize human well-being, equality and social justice. These values serve as a foundation for their pursuit of happiness, as they believe that a just and equitable society contributes to individual and collective happiness.

**Rationality and Critical Thinking:** Atheists often rely on rationality and critical thinking to assess their beliefs and life choices. They apply these skills to identify sources of unhappiness, make informed decisions and navigate life's challenges effectively.

**Authenticity:** Authenticity is a cornerstone of atheist approaches to happiness. Being true to oneself, living in alignment with one's values and expressing genuine emotions are seen as pathways to a more fulfilling life.

**Personal Growth and Fulfillment:** Atheists view personal growth and self-improvement as essential components of happiness. They set goals, seek new experiences and continuously strive to become the best version of themselves.

**Human Connection:** Human connection and relationships are central to atheist happiness. Building meaningful connections with others, fostering empathy and engaging in acts of kindness contribute to their sense of well-being.

**Pursuit of Knowledge:** The pursuit of knowledge and intellectual engagement is a source of happiness for many atheists. They find joy in learning, exploring new ideas and gaining a deeper understanding of the world.

**Gratitude and Appreciation:** Just as with gratitude, atheists appreciate the beauty and goodness in everyday life. They consciously cultivate gratitude for the simple pleasures, which can lead to greater overall happiness.

**Optimism and Resilience:** Atheists often approach life with optimism and resilience. They believe in the capacity of individuals and society to overcome challenges, which can lead to a more positive outlook and increased happiness.

**Purpose and Meaning:** Finding purpose and meaning in life is a shared pursuit among atheists. They often seek to make a positive impact on the world, contribute to causes they believe in and derive meaning from their actions.

**Balancing Hedonism and Eudaimonia:** Atheists navigate the balance between hedonistic pleasure and eudaimonic well-being. While they seek moments of joy and pleasure, they also recognize the importance of pursuing activities that contribute to their long-term flourishing and happiness.

**Self-Care and Well-Being:** Atheists prioritize self-care and well-being. They understand the importance of physical and mental health in achieving happiness and make efforts to maintain a balanced and healthy lifestyle.

In the pursuit of happiness, atheists draw on a combination of rationality, empathy, authenticity and a commitment to values that prioritize human flourishing. Their approaches to happiness are grounded in the belief that a fulfilling life is achievable through personal growth, meaningful relationships and a positive impact on the world.

# Chapter 17: Atheism and Social Justice

Atheism isn't just about the disbelief in deities; it often goes hand in hand with a commitment to social justice. Let's explore how atheists engage with social justice issues and why these matters are important to them.

**Humanism and Social Justice:** Many atheists identify as humanists, emphasizing the value and dignity of every human being. Humanism often leads to a strong commitment to social justice, advocating for equal rights and opportunities for all.

**Equality and Equity:** Atheists are often staunch advocates for equality and equity. They work to dismantle systemic discrimination and address the social, economic and political disparities that affect marginalized communities.

**Secular Ethics:** Atheists often derive their ethical principles from secular sources, such as reason, empathy and the well-being of humanity. These principles guide their advocacy for social justice, as they seek to create a fair and just society based on humanistic values.

**Separation of Church and State:** Many atheists emphasize the importance of a strict separation between religion and government. They argue that this separation is essential for upholding individual freedoms and preventing religious institutions from impeding progress in social justice.

**Secular Activism:** Atheists engage in various forms of activism to promote social justice. They work on issues like LGBTQ+ rights, gender equality, racial justice, reproductive rights and more, often collaborating with secular and non-religious organizations.

**LGBTQ+ Rights:** Atheists are often strong allies in the fight for LGBTQ+ rights. They advocate for equal rights, nondiscrimination and the recognition of diverse gender and sexual orientations.

**Women's Rights:** Atheists often support women's rights and gender equality, including access to reproductive healthcare, equal pay and protections against gender-based violence and discrimination.

**Racial Justice:** Atheists engage in discussions and activism related to racial justice. They work to address systemic racism, promote diversity and support policies that aim to reduce racial disparities.

**Environmental Justice:** Concerns about climate change and environmental justice are shared by many atheists. They advocate for sustainable practices and policies that protect the environment and vulnerable communities.

**Community Building:** Atheists often build communities that provide support and resources for marginalized groups. These communities create spaces where individuals can find acceptance and advocate for their rights.

**Challenging Religious Privilege:** Some atheists view religious privilege as a barrier to social justice. They work to challenge religious institutions that perpetuate discrimination and influence public policy.

**Intersectionality:** Atheists recognize that social justice issues are often interconnected. They embrace an intersectional approach, understanding that individuals may face multiple forms of discrimination and oppression simultaneously.

So atheism is not solely a rejection of religious belief; it's often accompanied by a commitment to social justice and humanistic values. Atheists advocate for equality, equity and the well-being of all individuals, working to create a more just and inclusive society.

# Chapter 18: Building a Supportive Atheist Community

Atheism can sometimes be a solitary belief, but many atheists find strength, companionship and support by connecting with like-minded individuals. Let's explore the importance of building and nurturing a supportive atheist community.

**Creating a Sense of Belonging:** One of the primary benefits of an atheist community is the sense of belonging it provides. It can be comforting to interact with others who share similar beliefs and values, especially in regions where religiosity is prevalent.

**Providing Emotional Support:** Atheist communities offer a safe space for individuals to share their thoughts, concerns and personal experiences without fear of judgment or discrimination. Emotional support from peers can be invaluable, especially during challenging times.

**Fostering Critical Thinking:** Atheist communities often encourage critical thinking and open dialogue. They provide opportunities for members to engage in thoughtful discussions, explore philosophical questions and challenge their own beliefs.

**Promoting Secular Values:** Atheist communities often rally around secular values such as reason, science and humanism. These values are shared and celebrated, reinforcing a sense of identity and purpose.

**Organizing Events and Activities:** Many atheist communities organize events, meetings and social activities. These gatherings provide opportunities for members to connect on a personal level, develop friendships and form a sense of community.

**Advocacy and Activism:** Atheist communities frequently engage in advocacy and activism related to secularism, church-state separation and social justice. Working together toward common goals can be empowering and fulfilling.

**Education and Outreach:** Some atheist communities focus on education and outreach. They aim to dispel myths and misconceptions about atheism, promote understanding and provide resources for those questioning their beliefs.

**Supporting Secular Causes:** Atheist communities often support secular causes, including organizations that defend the rights of non-religious individuals, promote secular education and advance scientific literacy.

**Addressing Stigma and Discrimination:** In regions where atheism may be stigmatized or misunderstood, atheist communities can serve as a support network for individuals facing discrimination or social challenges.

**Online Communities:** In the digital age, online atheist communities have become increasingly important. These forums provide a platform for individuals to connect globally, share information and find support from a diverse range of perspectives.

**Diversity and Inclusion:** Many atheist communities actively strive for diversity and inclusion. They recognize the importance of representing a broad spectrum of backgrounds, identities and experiences within their ranks.

**Support for Non-Believers in Religious Families:** Some atheist communities offer specialized support for individuals who are non-believers in religious families, helping them navigate complex family dynamics.

So atheist communities play a vital role in providing emotional support, fostering critical thinking and promoting secular values. They create spaces where individuals can connect, share experiences and work together to address common challenges and advance the principles they hold dear.

# Chapter 19: Atheist Perspectives on Love and Relationships

Love and relationships are central to the human experience and atheists approach these aspects of life with their own unique perspectives and values. Let's explore how atheists view love and cultivate meaningful relationships.

**Secular Love and Values:** Atheists often base their approach to love and relationships on secular values such as empathy, compassion and reason. They believe that love should be grounded in a deep understanding and respect for one another, rather than influenced by religious doctrines.

**Equality and Partnership:** In atheist relationships, equality and partnership are fundamental principles. They view relationships as a collaboration between equal partners, where decisions are made collectively and power dynamics are balanced.

**Emphasis on Communication:** Effective communication is a cornerstone of atheist relationships. Open and honest dialogue is encouraged, allowing partners to express their thoughts, feelings and concerns openly without fear of judgment.

**Shared Values:** While atheists may come from diverse backgrounds, they often seek partners who share their values and worldviews. Shared beliefs, ethics and goals provide a strong foundation for meaningful connections.

**Secular Weddings and Commitment:** Many atheists opt for secular weddings and commitment ceremonies that focus on their love and dedication to each other without religious rituals. These ceremonies often emphasize personal vows and the importance of their relationship in a secular context.

**Monogamy and Ethical Non-Monogamy:** Atheists have a range of views on relationship structures. Some choose monogamy, while others explore ethical non-monogamous relationships with the consent and communication of all parties involved.

**Respect for Autonomy:** In atheist relationships, individual autonomy and personal growth are highly respected. Partners encourage each other to pursue their passions, interests and personal development.

**Supporting Diversity:** Atheists often support diverse relationships and families. They advocate for LGBTQ+ rights, gender equality and recognition of a wide range of relationship orientations and identities.

**Responsibility and Accountability:** In the absence of religious moral frameworks, atheists often hold themselves accountable for their actions within relationships. They take responsibility for their behavior and seek to resolve conflicts constructively.

**Human Connection:** Above all, atheists value the deep human connection that love and relationships offer. They believe that love transcends religious boundaries and serves as a universal, deeply human experience.

**Family and Parenting:** For atheist parents, instilling secular values in their children is important. They often prioritize critical thinking, empathy and respect for diversity in their parenting approach.

**Respect for Consent:** Consent is a non-negotiable aspect of atheist relationships. Partners respect each other's boundaries and ensure that all intimate interactions are consensual.

So love and relationships in the atheist perspective are rooted in secular values, open communication and mutual respect. While religious beliefs may not play a role in their relationships, atheists place a strong emphasis on equality, autonomy and the deep human connection that love brings.

# Chapter 20: Atheism and Personal Growth

Atheism is more than just a disbelief in deities; it's often a journey of personal growth, self-discovery and continuous learning. Let's explore how atheism can be a catalyst for personal growth and development.

**Questioning and Critical Thinking:** Many atheists arrive at their non-belief through a process of questioning and critical thinking. This intellectual curiosity doesn't stop with the rejection of religion; it becomes a lifelong pursuit of knowledge and understanding.

**Embracing Uncertainty:** Atheism often means embracing uncertainty about the afterlife and the existence of a higher power. This acceptance of life's uncertainties can lead to personal growth by fostering resilience and adaptability.

**Self-Reliance:** In the absence of divine guidance, atheists often place a strong emphasis on self-reliance. They learn to trust their own judgment, make decisions independently and take responsibility for their actions.

**Moral Development:** Atheists often engage in moral and ethical reflection to determine their values and principles. This process of moral development can lead to a deeper understanding of one's beliefs and a commitment to living an ethical life.

**Empathy and Compassion:** Many atheists adopt humanistic values that emphasize empathy and compassion for others. These values drive personal growth by encouraging individuals to understand and connect with people from diverse backgrounds and perspectives.

**Interconnectedness:** Atheists may find a sense of interconnectedness with all living beings and the natural world, leading to personal growth by fostering a sense of responsibility and care for the environment and humanity.

**Challenging Stereotypes:** Living as an atheist in a predominantly religious society often involves challenging stereotypes and misconceptions. This process can lead to personal growth by promoting critical thinking and empathy.

**Advocacy and Activism:** Atheists often engage in advocacy and activism for secularism, social justice and the separation of church and state. These efforts provide opportunities for personal growth by empowering individuals to make a positive impact on society.

**Tolerance and Inclusivity:** In their interactions with people of diverse beliefs, atheists often practice tolerance and inclusivity. These values can lead to personal growth by broadening one's perspective and promoting understanding.

**Exploration of Worldviews:** Some atheists explore alternative worldviews, philosophies and spiritual practices as part of their personal growth journey. This exploration can provide new insights and perspectives.

**Resilience:** Facing potential social stigma or discrimination due to their atheism can cultivate resilience and inner strength in atheists. Overcoming such challenges contributes to personal growth.

**Philosophical Inquiry:** Atheists often engage in philosophical inquiry, exploring questions about the nature of existence, morality and the meaning of life. These inquiries can lead to personal growth by encouraging introspection and reflection.

So atheism can be a catalyst for personal growth, leading to greater intellectual curiosity, resilience, empathy and a commitment to living an ethical and meaningful life. The journey of self-discovery and continuous learning is a central aspect of the atheist experience.

# Chapter 21: Atheist Parenting: Raising Ethical Children

Atheist parents, like parents of all belief systems, face the rewarding challenge of raising ethical, compassionate and well-rounded children. Let's explore how atheist parents approach parenting and instill values in their children.

**Secular Values:** Atheist parents often base their parenting approach on secular values, emphasizing empathy, reason and critical thinking. They aim to instill these values in their children from a young age.

**Teaching Ethics:** Ethical discussions are common in atheist households. Parents engage their children in conversations about right and wrong, often encouraging them to think through moral dilemmas and make informed decisions.

**Encouraging Curiosity:** Atheist parents nurture their children's curiosity and love of learning. They encourage questions, exploration and the pursuit of knowledge, promoting intellectual growth.

**Promoting Empathy:** Empathy is a key value in atheist parenting. Parents teach their children to understand and share the feelings of others, fostering a sense of compassion and connection to the broader human experience.

**Encouraging Critical Thinking:** Critical thinking skills are highly valued by atheist parents. They encourage their children to question, analyze and evaluate information and ideas, enabling them to make reasoned decisions.

**Respect for Diversity:** Atheist parents often promote respect for diversity in all its forms, including religious, cultural and gender diversity. They teach their children to appreciate differences and treat others with respect.

**Science and Reason:** Many atheist parents emphasize the importance of science and reason in understanding the world. They encourage their children to embrace evidence-based thinking and critical reasoning.

**Balancing Autonomy and Guidance:** Atheist parents strike a balance between allowing their children autonomy to make choices and providing guidance. They aim to nurture independent thinking while offering support when needed.

**Secular Celebrations:** In atheist households, celebrations often have secular or humanistic themes. These events provide opportunities for parents to reinforce values and create lasting memories.

**Secular Education:** Some atheist parents choose secular education for their children, emphasizing critical thinking and secular ethics in their learning.

**Community Involvement:** Many atheist parents involve their children in secular or community service activities. This involvement helps children develop a sense of social responsibility and empathy for others.

**Promoting Ethical Behavior:** Above all, atheist parents strive to raise children who make ethical choices independently. They provide guidance and model ethical behavior, allowing their children to develop their moral compass.

**Parenting Without Fear:** Atheist parents often raise their children without the fear of religious punishment or judgment. Instead, they focus on teaching right from wrong based on secular values.

**Addressing Questions About Religion:** If their children have questions about religion, atheist parents often answer them honestly and objectively, allowing their children to form their own conclusions.

So atheist parenting centers on fostering ethical, empathetic and intellectually curious children. Atheist parents emphasize secular values, critical thinking and respect for diversity as they guide their children toward making informed and compassionate choices in their lives.

# Chapter 22: Art, Creativity and Atheist Expression

Art and creativity are universal human outlets for expression and atheists are no exception. Let's explore how atheists engage with art and creativity as a means of self-expression and connection with the world.

**Secular Inspiration:** Atheist artists often draw inspiration from the natural world, human experiences and the marvels of science. They find wonder in the beauty of the universe and the intricacies of life on Earth.

**Exploration of Existence:** Atheist artists may use their work as a way to explore questions about existence, meaning and the human condition. Through their art, they engage in philosophical and existential inquiries.

**Embracing Diversity:** Many atheist artists celebrate diversity in their work, recognizing the richness of human experiences, backgrounds and perspectives. They use their art to advocate for inclusivity and social justice.

**Challenging Norms:** Atheist artists sometimes use their creativity to challenge societal norms, including religious conventions and beliefs. They employ satire, irony and symbolism to critique and provoke thought.

**Humanism and Compassion:** Art created by atheists often reflects humanistic values, emphasizing compassion, empathy and a commitment to the well-being of humanity. They may use their art to shed light on social issues and inspire positive change.

**Promoting Rational Thought:** Some atheist artists use their creativity to promote rational thought and scientific literacy. Their art may aim to demystify misconceptions and encourage evidence-based thinking.

**Fostering Dialogue:** Art can be a powerful tool for fostering dialogue and understanding. Atheist artists sometimes use their work to initiate conversations about atheism, secularism and the separation of church and state.

**Interconnectedness:** Atheist artists may explore the idea of interconnectedness, highlighting the unity of all living beings and the environment. Their art often encourages viewers to reflect on our place in the natural world.

**Celebrating Life:** For many atheists, art is a celebration of life itself. They use their creativity to capture the vibrancy, diversity and complexity of the human experience, finding joy in the here and now.

**Secular Rituals:** Atheist artists sometimes create secular rituals and ceremonies that mark important life events, such as weddings, memorials and rites of passage. These rituals are designed to be meaningful without religious elements.

**Community Engagement:** Art can serve as a means of community engagement for atheists. They organize and participate in art-related events, exhibitions and projects that bring people together around shared themes and values.

**Personal Expression:** Above all, art and creativity are outlets for personal expression among atheists. Whether through visual arts, music, literature, or other mediums, they use their creativity to communicate their unique perspectives and experiences.

In essence, art and creativity are integral to the human experience and atheists use these forms of expression to explore the world, celebrate life, promote rational thought and engage with important social and philosophical questions. Their art reflects their values, perspectives and a deep connection with the wonders of the natural world.

# Chapter 23: Atheist Views on Mind-Body Connection

The relationship between the mind and body is a topic of significant interest and exploration among atheists. Let's delve into how atheists perceive the mind-body connection and its implications for their worldview.

**Naturalistic Perspective:** Atheists generally adopt a naturalistic worldview, which means they see the mind and body as products of natural processes without the need for supernatural explanations. They attribute mental processes to physical phenomena in the brain.

**Emphasis on Physicalism:** Many atheists align with physicalism, the philosophical position that all mental phenomena can be ultimately explained by physical processes. They believe that consciousness and cognitive functions arise from the activity of neurons and the brain's complex architecture.

**No Dualism:** Atheists tend to reject dualism, the idea that the mind and body are distinct substances. Instead, they see the mind as an emergent property of the physical brain, with no separate or immaterial aspect.

**Psychological Science:** Atheists often have a strong appreciation for psychological science and its role in understanding the mind. They view psychology and neuroscience as valuable tools for exploring the intricacies of human consciousness and behavior.

**Mental Health:** Atheists recognize the importance of mental health and well-being. They often advocate for evidence-based approaches to mental health care, including therapy, medication and support networks.

**Self-Identity:** Atheists generally see self-identity as a product of the brain's functioning. They believe that personal characteristics, memories and experiences are shaped by the physical processes occurring in the brain.

**Ethical Implications:** Some atheists argue that a naturalistic view of the mind-body connection has ethical implications. They emphasize the importance of personal responsibility for one's actions, as they see behavior as a result of both biological and environmental factors.

**Spirituality and the Mind:** While atheists may not attribute spiritual experiences to a supernatural realm, they acknowledge that the human mind can produce experiences that are often described as spiritual. These experiences are seen as products of brain activity and psychology.

**Materialism and Consumerism:** Atheists may be critical of materialistic and consumerist cultures that prioritize the accumulation of material possessions over mental and emotional well-being. They often advocate for a more balanced approach to life.

**Secular Ethics and Morality:** Atheists frequently base their ethical and moral values on secular principles, emphasizing empathy, reason and the well-being of others. They see ethical behavior as rooted in the mind's capacity for empathy and moral reasoning.

So atheists approach the mind-body connection from a naturalistic and physicalist perspective. They view the mind as an emergent property of the physical brain and they emphasize the importance of psychological science, mental health and ethical behavior in their worldview. While they may not attribute spiritual experiences to the supernatural, they acknowledge the complexity and wonder of the human mind.

# Chapter 24: The Science of Well-Being

Well-being, the state of being happy, healthy and content, is a fundamental pursuit for people of all belief systems, including atheists. Let's explore how atheists approach well-being through the lens of science and secular principles.

**Positive Psychology:** Atheists often draw from positive psychology, a scientific field focused on understanding and promoting human well-being. This approach emphasizes factors such as positive emotions, engagement, relationships, meaning and accomplishment.

**Emphasis on Evidence-Based Practices:** Atheists favor evidence-based practices for enhancing well-being. They look to scientific research to identify strategies and interventions that have been proven effective in promoting happiness and life satisfaction.

**Physical Health:** Atheists recognize the importance of physical health in overall well-being. They prioritize exercise, proper nutrition and healthcare as means of promoting physical and mental health.

**Mental Health Support:** Atheists place a strong emphasis on mental health support. They are proponents of seeking professional help when needed and reducing the stigma associated with mental health issues.

**Social Connections:** Building and maintaining meaningful social connections is central to atheist approaches to well-being. They value friendships, family relationships and community involvement as sources of support and happiness.

**Life Satisfaction:** Atheists often measure well-being by life satisfaction and overall happiness rather than relying on religious or supernatural notions of fulfillment. They look to secular sources of joy and contentment in their lives.

**Personal Growth:** Atheists are dedicated to personal growth and self-improvement. They engage in lifelong learning, set goals and seek experiences that contribute to their personal development.

**Resilience:** Building resilience to cope with life's challenges is a key aspect of atheist well-being. They recognize that setbacks are a part of life and aim to develop the emotional strength to bounce back from adversity.

**Pursuit of Meaning:** While atheists may not seek meaning in religious doctrines, they are passionate about finding personal meaning and purpose in life. They often derive meaning from relationships, contributions to society and personal achievements.

**Ethical Living:** Living ethically and in accordance with secular values is considered a source of well-being for atheists. They find fulfillment in contributing positively to society and promoting fairness, justice and compassion.

**Balancing Hedonism and Eudaimonia:** Atheists often aim to strike a balance between seeking immediate pleasure (hedonism) and pursuing long-term well-being and fulfillment (eudaimonia). They recognize that both elements are essential for a well-rounded life.

So atheists approach well-being from a secular and evidence-based perspective. They draw from fields such as positive psychology, emphasize physical and mental health, nurture social connections and seek personal growth and meaning in their pursuit of happiness and contentment.

# Chapter 25: Atheism and the Search for Truth

The pursuit of truth, knowledge and understanding is a common thread among atheists. Let's explore how atheists approach the quest for truth and how their worldview influences their search for knowledge.

**Rational Inquiry:** Atheists often engage in rational inquiry as a means to uncover truth. They rely on critical thinking, reason and evidence-based methods to examine claims, beliefs and the natural world.

**Scientific Inquiry:** Science is a cornerstone of atheist approaches to truth. Many atheists value the scientific method as a reliable tool for discovering knowledge about the universe, including its origins and workings.

**Skepticism:** Skepticism is a fundamental aspect of atheist thinking. Atheists are often naturally skeptical and question claims, especially those that lack empirical evidence or seem to contradict established scientific principles.

**Religious and Supernatural Claims:** Atheists critically evaluate religious and supernatural claims, often finding them lacking in empirical evidence. They maintain a stance of disbelief in gods and the supernatural until sufficient evidence is provided.

**Secular Ethics and Morality:** Atheists seek to understand the nature of ethics and morality from a secular perspective. They explore how moral values and principles can be grounded in reason, empathy and the well-being of humanity.

**Philosophical Inquiry:** Many atheists engage in philosophical inquiry to explore fundamental questions about existence, meaning and morality. They use philosophical frameworks to examine complex issues and to gain a deeper understanding of the human condition.

**Open-Mindedness:** While atheists tend to approach claims with skepticism, they also value open-mindedness. They are willing to consider new evidence and revise their beliefs in the light of compelling data.

**Ethical Responsibility:** Atheists often feel an ethical responsibility to seek truth and promote understanding. They believe that knowledge and evidence should guide decision-making and ethical behavior.

**Secular Worldview:** Atheists often construct a secular worldview based on naturalistic explanations for phenomena. They see the natural world as the primary source of knowledge and reject supernatural or mystical explanations.

**Exploration of Diverse Perspectives:** Atheists actively seek out and explore diverse perspectives, including those that challenge their own beliefs. They value intellectual diversity and the opportunity to engage in constructive dialogue.

**Secular Education:** Many atheists prioritize secular education as a means to foster critical thinking, scientific literacy and a well-rounded understanding of the world. They often advocate for evidence-based education in schools.

**Promoting Evidence-Based Thinking:** Atheists promote evidence-based thinking not only for themselves but also in wider society. They encourage others to rely on empirical evidence and rationality when making decisions and forming beliefs.

So atheists are committed to the search for truth and understanding, relying on rationality, skepticism and evidence-based methods to uncover knowledge about the natural world and the human experience. They approach claims, beliefs and moral questions with a critical yet open-minded perspective, seeking to contribute to a more informed and enlightened society.

# Chapter 26: Atheist Perspectives on Enlightenment

Enlightenment, broadly defined as the state of gaining deep understanding and insight, is a concept that resonates with atheists in various ways. Let's explore how atheists perceive and pursue enlightenment in their lives.

**Secular Enlightenment:** For atheists, enlightenment is often a secular pursuit, centered on gaining knowledge, wisdom and understanding through reason, empirical evidence and critical thinking. They seek enlightenment without relying on religious or supernatural explanations.

**The Role of Education:** Education is a powerful means of achieving enlightenment for atheists. They value formal education, self-directed learning and intellectual curiosity as pathways to deeper understanding.

**Scientific Enlightenment:** Many atheists view scientific exploration and discovery as a form of enlightenment. Science offers insights into the natural world, uncovering the mysteries of the universe and human existence.

**Critical Thinking:** Critical thinking is a cornerstone of atheist approaches to enlightenment. Atheists apply rationality, skepticism and logical analysis to evaluate claims and beliefs, striving for a more accurate understanding of reality.

**Philosophical Inquiry:** Philosophy plays a significant role in the quest for enlightenment among atheists. They engage in philosophical inquiry to explore fundamental questions about existence, morality and the human condition.

**Ethical Enlightenment:** Atheists often pursue ethical enlightenment, seeking to understand the nature of ethics and morality from a secular perspective. They explore how moral values can be grounded in reason, empathy and the well-being of humanity.

**Open-Mindedness:** Atheists value open-mindedness as a means of achieving enlightenment. They are willing to consider diverse perspectives and evidence, even if it challenges their existing beliefs.

**Empirical Enlightenment:** Atheists emphasize empirical evidence as a source of enlightenment. They rely on data, observation and the scientific method to gain a deeper understanding of the world.

**Promoting Enlightenment in Society:** Atheists often advocate for the promotion of enlightenment values in society, such as reason, evidence-based thinking and scientific literacy. They believe that an enlightened society is one that values knowledge, critical thinking and ethical behavior.

**Secular Wisdom:** Wisdom is highly regarded by atheists as a form of enlightenment. They seek to cultivate wisdom through life experiences, reflection and a commitment to personal growth.

**Questioning Authority:** Atheists often question authority and challenge established norms and beliefs as part of their pursuit of enlightenment. They recognize the importance of independent thinking and skepticism.

**Contributing to Knowledge:** Atheists actively contribute to human knowledge and enlightenment by engaging in research, scientific discovery and intellectual discourse. They see the dissemination of knowledge as a means of advancing society.

So enlightenment for atheists is a secular and rational pursuit of knowledge, wisdom and understanding. It encompasses scientific exploration, critical thinking, ethical reflection and a commitment to open-mindedness. Atheists believe that enlightenment leads to a deeper appreciation of the natural world and a more informed and enlightened society.

# Chapter 27: Atheism and Existentialism

Existentialism is a philosophical movement that explores themes related to existence, freedom, choice and the search for meaning in an inherently indifferent universe. Let's delve into how atheists often intersect with existentialist ideas and themes.

**Absence of Divine Meaning:** One of the key intersections between atheism and existentialism is the recognition of the absence of divine or predetermined meaning in life. Atheists, by rejecting theism, often align with the existentialist view that life's meaning must be constructed or discovered by individuals themselves.

**Freedom and Responsibility:** Existentialism places a strong emphasis on individual freedom and responsibility for one's choices. Atheists similarly embrace the idea that they are responsible for their actions and decisions in the absence of divine guidance or determinism.

**Creating Meaning:** Both atheists and existentialists grapple with the question of how to create meaning in a seemingly indifferent universe. They acknowledge that individuals have the capacity to imbue their lives with personal significance through their choices and actions.

**Authenticity:** Existentialists encourage authenticity, the idea of living in accordance with one's true self and values. Atheists often value authenticity as well, emphasizing the importance of being true to oneself and one's beliefs.

**Facing Absurdity:** Existentialists confront the concept of the absurd, the realization that life lacks inherent meaning or purpose. Atheists, in rejecting religious narratives, often grapple with similar feelings of existential absurdity.

**Ethical Concerns:** Existentialism often explores ethical questions and atheists engage in ethical inquiry as well. Both groups consider questions of morality and how individuals should behave in a universe devoid of divine moral guidance.

**Embracing Uncertainty:** Existentialism encourages individuals to embrace the uncertainty and ambiguity of life. Atheists, too, acknowledge the inherent uncertainty of existence and seek ways to navigate it with courage and authenticity.

**Living in the Here and Now:** Existentialist philosophy often emphasizes the importance of living in the present moment rather than fixating on an imagined future or dwelling on the past. Many atheists adopt a similar perspective, valuing the present as the locus of meaning and action.

**Creating One's Values:** Existentialists propose that individuals must create their own values and ethics. Atheists often embrace this idea, striving to develop ethical systems based on reason, empathy and the well-being of humanity.

**Resilience and Strength:** Existentialism encourages individuals to confront life's challenges with resilience and inner strength. Atheists, facing potential stigma or discrimination, often cultivate resilience and fortitude in their pursuit of a meaningful life.

**Intellectual Exploration:** Both existentialists and atheists value intellectual exploration and critical thinking. They engage in philosophical inquiry to better understand the complexities of existence and the human condition.

So existentialist themes resonate with many atheists, as both groups grapple with questions of existence, meaning, freedom and responsibility in a world without divine guidance. While not all atheists identify as existentialists, they often find common ground in the exploration of these philosophical concepts and their application to the secular human experience.

# Chapter 28: The Role of Literature in Atheist Spirituality

Literature, in its various forms, has the power to evoke deep emotions, provoke contemplation and offer profound insights into the human experience. For atheists, literature can play a significant role in their exploration of spirituality, meaning and the complexities of life in a secular context. Let's examine the role of literature in atheist spirituality.

**Exploring Life's Questions:** Literature often delves into existential questions about life, death, morality and the nature of existence. Atheists, like all individuals, grapple with these questions and literature provides a platform for exploring different perspectives and interpretations.

**Emotional Connection:** Well-crafted literature can evoke a wide range of emotions, allowing atheists to connect with the depth of human experience. They may find solace, empathy, or inspiration in the stories and characters they encounter.

**Moral Reflection:** Literature frequently raises ethical dilemmas and moral issues. Atheists, who often base their ethics on secular principles, can use literature as a tool for moral reflection, considering how characters' choices and consequences relate to their own ethical beliefs.

**Humanism and Empathy:** Many atheist readers appreciate literature that promotes humanism and empathy. They resonate with stories that emphasize the inherent worth and dignity of individuals, regardless of religious beliefs.

**Existential Exploration:** Existentialist literature, which grapples with questions of meaning, freedom and responsibility, often resonates with atheists. These works can mirror the atheists' own philosophical explorations.

**Critical Thinking:** Literature can challenge readers to think critically about complex issues. Atheists value critical thinking as a means to evaluate claims, beliefs and worldviews and literature can serve as a source of intellectual stimulation.

**Community and Discussion:** Atheists may engage in book clubs or discussion groups focused on secular and philosophical literature. These forums provide opportunities for communal exploration of deep questions and the sharing of diverse perspectives.

**Personal Growth:** Literature can contribute to personal growth and self-discovery. Atheists often seek to develop their understanding of the world and themselves and literature can be a valuable tool in this journey.

**Inspiration for Creativity:** Literature, including poetry and fiction, can inspire creativity among atheists. They may draw upon the themes, symbolism and narratives they encounter in literature to express their own ideas and experiences.

**Questioning Authority:** Atheists, who often question religious authority and dogma, may appreciate literature that challenges societal norms and authority figures, encouraging readers to think independently and critically.

**Narratives of Non-Belief:** Some literature explores the experiences of individuals who reject religious belief. Atheists may identify with these narratives, finding resonance with characters who navigate life without reliance on the supernatural.

So literature holds a special place in the lives of many atheists, offering a platform for exploring life's complexities, ethical dilemmas and existential questions. It provides a means of emotional connection, intellectual stimulation and personal growth in the context of atheist spirituality, which is often grounded in reason, empathy and the secular human experience.

# Chapter 29: Atheism and Environmentalism

Environmentalism, the advocacy for the protection and preservation of the natural world, is a cause that resonates with many atheists. Let's explore the connections between atheism and environmentalism and how secular worldviews often align with the values of environmental stewardship.

**Secular Ethics and Environmental Concerns:** Atheists often base their ethical values on secular principles, emphasizing empathy, reason and the well-being of humanity. These values naturally extend to concerns about the environment and the impact of human activities on the planet.

**Naturalistic Worldview:** Many atheists embrace a naturalistic worldview, which recognizes the interconnectedness of all life forms and ecosystems. This perspective underscores the importance of preserving the environment for the well-being of future generations.

**Scientific Understanding:** Atheists tend to value scientific understanding and rely on scientific evidence to make informed decisions. They recognize the scientific consensus on climate change and environmental degradation, motivating them to take action.

**Rejecting Divine Dominion:** Atheists often reject the idea of divine dominion, which asserts that humans have a divine right to dominate and exploit the Earth. Instead, they advocate for responsible and sustainable interactions with the environment.

**Advocacy for Conservation:** Many atheist individuals and organizations actively advocate for conservation efforts, habitat protection and the preservation of biodiversity. They see these actions as essential for maintaining the health of the planet.

**Secular Environmental Ethics:** Atheists may develop secular environmental ethics based on rational considerations, ecological principles and the recognition of the intrinsic value of nature. They promote values such as sustainability, ecological responsibility and environmental justice.

**Secular Spirituality in Nature:** Some atheists find a form of secular spirituality in nature itself. They appreciate the beauty, wonder and complexity of the natural world and feel a deep sense of connection to it.

**Addressing Environmental Challenges:** Atheists often engage in discussions and activism to address environmental challenges, including climate change, pollution, deforestation and species extinction. They view these issues as global crises that require urgent action.

**Promotion of Science-Based Solutions:** Atheists frequently advocate for science-based solutions to environmental problems. They support policies and initiatives that are grounded in scientific research and evidence.

**Education and Awareness:** Many atheists contribute to environmental education and awareness campaigns. They recognize the importance of informing the public about environmental issues and inspiring collective action.

**Global Responsibility:** Atheists often emphasize the global responsibility to address environmental problems. They recognize that environmental issues transcend national boundaries and require international cooperation.

**Eco-Friendly Lifestyles:** Atheists, like many environmentally conscious individuals, often adopt eco-friendly lifestyles. They make choices that reduce their environmental footprint, such as conserving energy, reducing waste and supporting sustainable practices.

So atheism and environmentalism often intersect through shared values of empathy, reason and a naturalistic worldview. Atheists advocate for responsible stewardship of the environment, recognizing the need to address pressing environmental challenges through science, ethics and collective action.

# Chapter 30: The Power of Atheist Symbols

Symbols have played a significant role in human culture, providing visual representation to complex ideas and belief systems. Atheism, despite its lack of centralized beliefs or religious dogma, has developed a range of symbols that hold meaning and serve various purposes within the atheist community. Let's explore the power of atheist symbols and their significance.

**The Atheist "A":** Perhaps one of the most recognizable symbols of atheism is the scarlet letter "A" enclosed within a circle. This symbol, popularized by organizations like the Richard Dawkins Foundation, serves as a simple yet effective way for atheists to identify themselves and express their non-belief. The "A" stands for atheism, but it also represents reason, logic and secularism.

**The Darwin Fish:** The Darwin fish is a play on the Christian fish symbol, incorporating legs and the name "Darwin" inside. It's often displayed on bumper stickers or badges by atheists who embrace evolutionary theory and science as a fundamental aspect of their worldview.

**The Flying Spaghetti Monster:** This humorous and satirical symbol represents the Flying Spaghetti Monster, a fictional deity created to critique the teaching of intelligent design and creationism in schools. It has become a symbol of atheistic skepticism toward supernatural claims.

**The Invisible Pink Unicorn:** Similar to the Flying Spaghetti Monster, the Invisible Pink Unicorn is a whimsical symbol used by atheists to highlight the absurdity of unfalsifiable claims about supernatural beings. It's a playful way to emphasize the need for evidence in belief.

**The Atom Symbol:** The atom symbol, often depicted with electrons orbiting the nucleus, represents science, rationality and the naturalistic worldview embraced by many atheists. It signifies a commitment to empirical evidence and the scientific method.

**Secular Humanism Symbols:** Secular humanism, a philosophy closely aligned with atheism, has its own symbols, including the Happy Human and the Secular Star. These symbols represent humanist values, including reason, compassion and ethical living.

**The Scarlet Letter "A" for Out Campaign:** The Out Campaign, initiated by prominent atheist Richard Dawkins, encourages atheists to "come out" and openly identify as non-believers. The scarlet letter "A" is a central symbol of this movement, signifying the act of declaring one's atheism.

**The Carl Sagan Baloney Detection Kit:** Named after the renowned astrophysicist and science communicator Carl Sagan, this symbol represents critical thinking and skepticism. It encourages atheists and others to apply rigorous reasoning to claims and beliefs.

**The Circle of Reason:** This symbol, a circle enclosing the word "reason," signifies the importance of rational thinking and evidence-based decision-making. It's a straightforward representation of the atheist commitment to reason.

**Personal Symbols:** Some atheists create their own personal symbols to represent their unique perspectives and experiences. These symbols may incorporate elements of nature, science, or personal symbolism that hold significance for the individual.

So atheist symbols serve as a visual means of expressing identity, values and beliefs within the atheist community. While atheism lacks centralized religious symbols, these secular symbols provide a way for atheists to communicate their worldview, promote critical thinking and challenge supernatural claims in a creative and often humorous manner. They also foster a sense of community and solidarity among atheists who may otherwise be isolated in predominantly religious societies.

# Chapter 31: Atheist Approaches to Healing

Healing, both physical and emotional, is a universal human concern that transcends religious and cultural boundaries. Atheists, like people of any belief system, seek ways to address pain, suffering and challenges in their lives. Let's explore how atheists approach healing and find meaning in the absence of religious or supernatural beliefs.

**Physical Healing and Medical Science:** Atheists generally place their trust in medical science and evidence-based healthcare for physical healing. They seek medical treatments, therapies and interventions to address health issues, emphasizing the importance of medical expertise and research.

**Mental Health and Psychological Well-Being:** Atheists recognize the importance of mental health and emotional well-being. They engage in therapies, counseling and support networks to address emotional challenges and promote psychological healing.

**Embracing Naturalism:** Atheists often embrace a naturalistic worldview, which can influence their approach to healing. They acknowledge the body's natural capacity to heal and recover and they may emphasize lifestyle choices that support physical and mental well-being.

**Mind-Body Connection:** Atheists may explore the mind-body connection, recognizing the impact of mental states on physical health and vice versa. Practices like meditation, mindfulness and stress reduction techniques are seen as ways to promote holistic healing.

**Human Connection and Empathy:** Atheists value human connection and empathy as important factors in healing. They may seek comfort, understanding and support from friends, family and social networks during times of difficulty.

**Narrative and Storytelling:** Atheists often find solace and healing through narrative and storytelling. Sharing personal experiences, expressing emotions and finding common ground with others can foster a sense of connection and provide a platform for healing.

**Coping Mechanisms:** Like individuals of any belief system, atheists develop coping mechanisms to navigate life's challenges. They may engage in creative activities, hobbies, physical exercise, or other practices that help them manage stress and find emotional healing.

**Resilience and Inner Strength:** Atheists often cultivate resilience and inner strength as a means of healing and coping with adversity. They recognize the need to confront challenges with courage and a positive mindset.

**Community Support:** Atheists may find healing within supportive communities of like-minded individuals. Whether through secular organizations, online forums, or local meetups, these communities offer a space for sharing experiences and finding understanding.

**Finding Meaning in Human Connections:** Atheists often derive meaning and healing from their relationships with other people. They recognize the power of human connection, empathy and compassion in the process of healing.

**Acceptance of Life's Imperfections:** Atheists may embrace the imperfections and uncertainties of life as part of the human experience. They find healing in accepting the ebb and flow of life and developing a sense of inner peace despite challenges.

So atheists approach healing through a combination of evidence-based medical practices, mental health support, naturalistic approaches, human connection and personal coping mechanisms. While they may not attribute healing to divine intervention, they draw on a range of strategies to address physical and emotional challenges and find meaning in their experiences.

# Chapter 32: Atheist Views on Community Service

Community service, the act of volunteering time and effort to benefit others and the community at large, is a practice that holds significance for many atheists. Let's explore atheist views on community service and how secular values motivate individuals to engage in acts of kindness and support for their communities.

**Human-Centered Values:** Atheists often base their ethical values on a human-centered approach, emphasizing the well-being and dignity of all individuals. This values-based perspective compels many atheists to engage in community service as a way to contribute positively to society.

**Compassion and Empathy:** Atheists, like people of any belief system, possess compassion and empathy for others. These qualities motivate them to offer assistance and support to those in need, recognizing the value of alleviating suffering and promoting human flourishing.

**Secular Ethics:** Many atheists develop secular ethical frameworks that guide their actions, including community service. They may derive their sense of moral responsibility from reason, empathy and a commitment to social justice.

**Social Responsibility:** Atheists often emphasize social responsibility as a fundamental aspect of their worldview. They recognize the importance of collective action to address societal challenges and disparities and community service is one way to contribute to positive change.

**Promoting Human Well-Being:** Acts of community service align with the atheist goal of promoting human well-being and improving the lives of individuals and communities. They see service as a means to enhance the quality of life for others.

**Local and Global Impact:** Atheists engage in community service at both local and global levels. They recognize that their efforts can have a positive impact on their immediate communities as well as on broader issues, such as poverty, education and public health.

**Advocacy for Secular Values:** Some atheists use community service as a platform for advocating secular values and demonstrating that individuals without religious beliefs can be moral and compassionate contributors to society.

**Voluntary Action:** Atheists often value the voluntary nature of community service. They believe that individuals should engage in acts of kindness and support out of their own free will and not as a result of religious obligation or coercion.

**Diversity and Inclusivity:** Atheists embrace diversity and inclusivity in their community service efforts. They recognize the importance of serving diverse populations and addressing the needs of individuals from all walks of life.

**Environmental Stewardship:** Atheists may engage in community service related to environmental conservation and sustainability. They view protecting the environment as a shared responsibility and contribute to efforts aimed at preserving natural resources.

**Critical Thinking in Service:** Atheists often apply critical thinking and evidence-based approaches to their community service efforts. They seek to make informed decisions about where their time and resources can have the greatest positive impact.

**Collective Action:** Atheists may join secular and humanist organizations that engage in community service as part of their mission. These groups provide a platform for atheists to collaborate with like-minded individuals in service of common goals.

So community service holds significant value for atheists who seek to make a positive impact on their communities and society at large. Their motivations are rooted in secular ethics, compassion and a commitment to the well-being of humanity. Atheists view community service as a way to demonstrate their values, promote social responsibility and contribute to a more inclusive and compassionate world.

# Chapter 33: Atheism and Global Perspectives

Atheism, as a worldview centered on the disbelief in deities, is not confined to any single culture or geographic region. It spans the globe and encompasses a diverse range of perspectives and experiences. Let's explore how atheism intersects with global perspectives and the ways in which atheists engage with and contribute to a worldwide community.

**Diversity of Atheist Experiences:** Atheism is not a monolithic belief system but rather a label that encompasses a wide spectrum of beliefs, backgrounds and experiences. Atheists come from various cultural, ethnic and linguistic backgrounds, contributing to a rich tapestry of global perspectives.

**Atheism Across Cultures:** Atheism exists in every corner of the world, challenging the assumption that religious belief is universal. Atheists in different cultures may face unique challenges and opportunities, influenced by the prevailing religious norms and social attitudes.

**Secular Humanism as a Global Ethical Framework:** Secular humanism, a philosophy closely aligned with atheism, offers a global ethical framework that transcends cultural boundaries. It emphasizes values such as reason, empathy and the well-being of humanity, providing a common ground for atheists from diverse backgrounds.

**Challenges to Atheism:** In some parts of the world, atheism can be met with resistance, discrimination, or even persecution. Atheists in these regions often work to promote freedom of thought and expression, advocating for secularism and the separation of religion from government.

**Global Atheist Organizations:** Atheists around the world have formed global and regional organizations to connect with like-minded individuals, provide support and engage in advocacy for secularism, reason and human rights.

**Atheist Activism:** Atheists engage in activism on global issues, such as promoting scientific literacy, advocating for freedom of speech and challenging religiously inspired laws and practices that infringe on human rights.

**Interfaith Dialogue:** Some atheists participate in interfaith dialogue as a means of fostering understanding and cooperation between religious and non-religious communities. They seek common ground on issues of mutual concern, such as social justice and ethics.

**Promoting Secular Values:** Atheists often work to promote secular values, such as the separation of church and state, religious neutrality in public policy and equal rights for all individuals, regardless of their beliefs.

**Global Challenges:** Atheists recognize the importance of addressing global challenges, including environmental sustainability, poverty, conflict resolution and public health. They collaborate with diverse groups to find solutions to these pressing issues.

**Cultural Sensitivity:** Atheists who engage in global perspectives often emphasize cultural sensitivity and respect for local customs and beliefs. They seek to build bridges and engage in constructive dialogue rather than impose their own worldview.

**International Solidarity:** Atheists may express solidarity with individuals and communities facing discrimination or persecution due to their non-religious beliefs. They advocate for freedom of thought and expression on a global scale.

**Supporting Global Education:** Many atheists support global education initiatives aimed at promoting critical thinking, scientific literacy and access to quality education for all, regardless of religious background.

So atheism is a global phenomenon that encompasses a diverse range of perspectives and experiences. Atheists from around the world engage with global issues, promote secular values and work towards a more inclusive and rational world. Their contributions to global perspectives extend beyond disbelief in deities to encompass human rights, ethics and the pursuit of a more equitable and compassionate global society.

# Chapter 34: Atheist Philosophy of Time

Time, with its inexorable flow and impact on human existence, has been a subject of philosophical inquiry for centuries. Atheists, who typically ground their worldview in reason and the natural world, have developed various philosophical perspectives on time. Let's delve into the atheist philosophy of time and how it intersects with questions of existence, purpose and meaning.

**Naturalistic Worldview:** Atheists often embrace a naturalistic worldview that asserts that the natural world is the only reality, devoid of supernatural forces or divine plans. This perspective influences their philosophy of time.

**Absence of Divine Plan:** Atheists reject the idea of a divine plan or preordained destiny. They see time as unfolding without the guidance of a higher power, leaving the course of events to be determined by natural processes and human agency.

**Embracing the Finite:** Atheists acknowledge the finitude of human life and the impermanence of all things. In this context, time takes on a precious quality, urging individuals to make the most of their limited existence.

**Temporal Relativity:** Atheists often appreciate the insights of scientific theories like relativity, which have reshaped our understanding of time. These theories challenge conventional notions of time as an absolute and uniform concept.

**Life's Evolving Nature:** Atheists may view time as a vehicle for life's evolution and development. They see the progression of time as the backdrop against which life adapts and changes in response to environmental and biological factors.

**Individual and Collective Histories:** Atheists value the importance of understanding individual and collective histories. They recognize that the events of the past shape the present and future, motivating them to study and learn from history.

**Moment-to-Moment Significance:** Many atheists embrace a philosophy of living in the present moment, emphasizing the significance of each passing instant. They find meaning and purpose in the experiences and interactions of daily life.

**Moral Responsibility:** Atheists may view the passage of time as a call to moral responsibility. They recognize that the consequences of actions extend into the future and seek to make ethical choices that positively impact the world.

**Ethical Living:** Some atheists adopt an ethical philosophy that prioritizes the well-being of individuals and society. They see time as an opportunity to work towards a more just and compassionate world.

**Legacy and Influence:** Atheists often contemplate the legacy they leave behind. They recognize that their actions and ideas can have a lasting impact on future generations, motivating them to contribute positively to human progress.

**Meaning-Making in a Natural World:** Atheists seek to find meaning and purpose in a world that lacks supernatural guidance. They may embrace secular philosophies, such as humanism, that emphasize the importance of creating meaning through human endeavors.

**Embracing Uncertainty:** Atheists often acknowledge the inherent uncertainty of the future. They find solace in embracing the unknown and navigating the complexities of life with courage and resilience.

So the atheist philosophy of time is shaped by a naturalistic worldview that emphasizes the absence of divine plans and the finitude of human existence. Atheists find meaning in the present moment, the evolution of life, ethical living and the legacy they leave behind. Their philosophy of time encourages them to embrace uncertainty and make the most of their limited time in the natural world.

# Chapter 35: The Art of Atheist Forgiveness

Forgiveness is a complex and deeply human experience that transcends religious and non-religious worldviews. Atheists, who often approach moral and ethical questions from a secular perspective, engage in the act of forgiveness guided by their own philosophical and emotional considerations. Let's explore the art of atheist forgiveness and how it intersects with reason, empathy and personal growth.

**Reason-Based Ethics:** Atheists often base their ethics on reason, empathy and the well-being of individuals and society. Forgiveness, in the atheist context, may be rooted in the rational recognition that holding onto anger and resentment can be detrimental to one's mental and emotional health.

**Empathy and Understanding:** Many atheists approach forgiveness with a strong sense of empathy and understanding. They recognize that people are fallible and understanding the motives and circumstances behind hurtful actions can be a path toward forgiveness.

**Personal Growth and Healing:** Forgiveness is often viewed as a means of personal growth and emotional healing by atheists. Letting go of grudges and anger can lead to greater emotional well-being and mental clarity.

**Accountability and Restitution:** Atheists may place a strong emphasis on accountability and restitution when considering forgiveness. They may require acknowledgment of wrongdoing and a genuine effort to make amends before extending forgiveness.

**Closure and Moving Forward:** Forgiveness for atheists can provide a sense of closure and a way to move forward from painful experiences. It allows them to release the emotional burden of past hurts and focus on the present and future.

**Setting Boundaries:** Some atheists view forgiveness as compatible with setting healthy boundaries. They may forgive but also take steps to protect themselves from further harm or manipulation.

**Conditional Forgiveness:** Atheists may engage in conditional forgiveness, where forgiveness is offered on the condition of certain criteria being met, such as genuine remorse or efforts to rectify the harm caused.

**Rejecting Divine Intervention:** In contrast to religious beliefs that may invoke divine intervention or divine forgiveness, atheists often reject the idea of divine forgiveness and see forgiveness as a human endeavor.

**Ethical Considerations:** Atheists may consider forgiveness as an ethical choice that aligns with their values of empathy and compassion. They may extend forgiveness as a way to promote ethical behavior and a more compassionate society.

**Facing Injustice:** Atheists may grapple with forgiveness in the face of injustice or harm caused by systemic issues or oppressive structures. They may focus on addressing societal issues while still working toward personal forgiveness.

**Individual and Cultural Variations:** Like forgiveness in religious contexts, atheist forgiveness can vary widely among individuals and across cultures. Atheists may draw on a diverse range of philosophies and emotional experiences when navigating forgiveness.

**Embracing Complexity:** The art of atheist forgiveness often acknowledges the complexity of human relationships and emotions. It recognizes that forgiveness can be a process and it may not always result in reconciliation.

So the art of atheist forgiveness is guided by reason, empathy, personal growth and ethical considerations. Atheists may engage in forgiveness as a means of healing and personal development, emphasizing the importance of understanding, accountability and setting boundaries. While forgiveness can be a deeply personal and sometimes challenging journey, it reflects the values of compassion and empathy within the atheist worldview.

# Chapter 36: Atheist Views on Technology and Progress

Atheists, who often ground their worldview in reason, evidence-based thinking and the natural world, hold diverse views on technology and progress. Let's explore how atheism intersects with perspectives on technological advancement and its impact on society, ethics and the future.

**Embracing Scientific Advancement:** Atheists tend to embrace scientific advancement as a means of understanding and improving the natural world. They see technology as a product of human ingenuity and scientific progress.

**Rational Approach:** Atheists often approach technology from a rational standpoint, emphasizing evidence-based decision-making and critical thinking. They support technological developments that are backed by scientific research and prioritize ethical considerations.

**Human-Centered Ethics:** Many atheists adopt human-centered ethics, valuing technology that enhances the well-being of individuals and society. They may view scientific and technological progress as a means of addressing human challenges and improving quality of life.

**Skepticism and Ethical Concerns:** While supportive of technology, atheists also maintain a healthy skepticism and raise ethical concerns about its potential misuse. They advocate for responsible and ethical technological development, particularly in areas like artificial intelligence, biotechnology and surveillance.

**Secular Ethical Frameworks:** Atheists often turn to secular ethical frameworks, such as secular humanism, to guide their views on technology and progress. These frameworks emphasize values like reason, compassion and the well-being of humanity.

**Promoting Education:** Atheists frequently support education and scientific literacy as a means of empowering individuals to make informed decisions about technology. They advocate for the importance of critical thinking skills in evaluating technological advancements.

**Championing Progress:** Many atheists champion progress as a way to address societal challenges, from healthcare and environmental sustainability to poverty alleviation and access to education. They see technology as a tool for advancing human progress and improving living conditions.

**Advocating for Ethical AI:** Atheists often engage in discussions and activism surrounding the ethical development and use of artificial intelligence (AI). They emphasize the need for AI systems that prioritize fairness, transparency and accountability.

**Environmental Responsibility:** Atheists recognize the importance of environmental responsibility in technological development. They advocate for sustainable and environmentally friendly technologies that mitigate harm to the planet.

**Evaluating Ethical Dilemmas:** Atheists may engage in ethical discussions about emerging technologies, such as genetic engineering or autonomous weapons. They consider the potential consequences and ethical dilemmas associated with these technologies.

**Human Rights and Technology:** Atheists often align with human rights principles when assessing technology's impact on society. They advocate for the protection of individual rights, including privacy and freedom of expression, in the digital age.

**Evaluating Technological Risks:** Atheists, like individuals of any belief system, evaluate the risks associated with technology. They seek to balance the benefits of technological progress with potential risks and unintended consequences.

So atheists approach technology and progress with a rational and human-centered perspective. They support scientific advancements that enhance well-being while advocating for responsible and ethical technological development. Atheists engage in discussions about the impact of technology on society, ethics and human rights, emphasizing the importance of critical thinking and ethical considerations in the ever-evolving world of technology.

# Chapter 37: Atheist Exploration of Altered States of Consciousness

Altered states of consciousness, which include experiences like meditation, lucid dreaming and psychedelic experiences, have fascinated humans throughout history. Atheists, who typically ground their worldview in naturalistic and evidence-based thinking, also explore these altered states, often from a secular and scientific perspective. Let's delve into how atheists approach and explore altered states of consciousness.

**Naturalistic Approach:** Atheists generally approach altered states of consciousness from a naturalistic standpoint, seeking to understand these phenomena through scientific inquiry and rational exploration.

**Lucid Dreaming:** Atheists may explore lucid dreaming, a state in which individuals become aware that they are dreaming and can sometimes exert control over their dream experiences. Lucid dreaming is seen as a natural phenomenon, not requiring supernatural explanations.

**Psychedelic Experiences:** Some atheists engage in responsible and informed use of psychedelics, such as psilocybin or LSD, to explore altered states of consciousness. They may be interested in the potential therapeutic or introspective benefits of these substances.

**Neuroscientific Inquiry:** Atheists often turn to neuroscience to explore altered states of consciousness. They seek to understand the neural mechanisms behind these experiences and how they relate to brain function.

**Exploration of Human Potential:** Atheists may view altered states of consciousness as a means of exploring the full range of human potential and consciousness. They seek to expand their understanding of the mind without resorting to supernatural explanations.

**Enhancing Well-Being:** Altered states of consciousness are sometimes explored by atheists as a way to enhance mental and emotional well-being. Practices like meditation and mindfulness are seen as tools for achieving greater life satisfaction.

**Mind-Body Connection:** Atheists often explore altered states in the context of the mind-body connection. They recognize that mental states can influence physical well-being and explore practices that promote holistic health.

**Philosophical Inquiry:** Altered states of consciousness can prompt philosophical inquiry among atheists. They may contemplate questions related to the nature of consciousness, selfhood and the boundaries of human perception.

**Ethical Considerations:** Atheists engage in discussions about the ethical use of altered states of consciousness, particularly in the context of psychedelics. They advocate for responsible and informed exploration, emphasizing safety and harm reduction.

**Scientific Research:** Some atheists are involved in scientific research on altered states of consciousness. They contribute to studies that investigate the potential benefits and risks of these experiences and their applications in various fields.

**Secular Spirituality:** For some atheists, altered states of consciousness are part of a secular spirituality that emphasizes personal growth, introspection and the exploration of the human experience without reliance on supernatural beliefs.

So atheists explore altered states of consciousness from a naturalistic and evidence-based perspective. They engage in practices like meditation and mindfulness, investigate the neuroscientific underpinnings of altered states and may responsibly explore the use of psychedelics. Altered states of consciousness are often seen as a means of enhancing well-being, expanding understanding and exploring the boundaries of human potential without resorting to supernatural explanations.

# Chapter 38: Atheism and Interfaith Dialogue

Interfaith dialogue, which involves discussions and cooperation between individuals of different religious backgrounds, is a concept that extends beyond the realm of religious belief. Atheists, who often identify as non-religious, also engage in interfaith dialogue, although their participation is characterized by a distinct perspective rooted in secularism, reason and humanism. Let's explore how atheists approach interfaith dialogue and its significance in fostering understanding and cooperation.

**Secular Engagement:** Atheists engage in interfaith dialogue from a secular standpoint, emphasizing shared human values, reason and ethics as common ground for discussion and collaboration.

**Promoting Understanding:** Atheists see interfaith dialogue as an opportunity to promote understanding and bridge gaps between religious and non-religious communities. They recognize that dialogue can break down stereotypes and misconceptions.

**Human-Centered Values:** Many atheists approach interfaith dialogue by emphasizing human-centered values, such as empathy, compassion and the well-being of individuals and society. They seek common ground in ethical principles that transcend religious beliefs.

**Ethical Collaboration:** Atheists may collaborate with religious groups on projects and initiatives that align with shared ethical goals, such as addressing poverty, promoting education, or advocating for social justice.

**Dialogue on Ethics:** Interfaith dialogue for atheists often centers on ethical discussions rather than theological debates. They explore questions of morality, social responsibility and human rights that are relevant to individuals of all beliefs.

**Building Bridges:** Atheists engage in interfaith dialogue to build bridges between communities and foster mutual respect. They believe that open and respectful communication can lead to more inclusive and harmonious societies.

**Religion and Secularism:** Interfaith dialogue allows atheists to engage in constructive conversations about the role of religion and secularism in public life. They advocate for a secular society that respects the freedom of belief and non-belief.

**Addressing Prejudice:** Atheists may use interfaith dialogue as a platform to address prejudice and discrimination against non-religious individuals. They seek to promote a more inclusive and tolerant society.

**Advocating for Secular Values:** In interfaith settings, atheists may advocate for secular values, such as the separation of church and state, religious neutrality in public policy and equal rights for individuals of all beliefs.

**Mutual Learning:** Atheists view interfaith dialogue as an opportunity for mutual learning. They are open to understanding the perspectives and experiences of individuals from diverse religious backgrounds.

**Community Engagement:** Atheists may engage with religious communities on community service projects, disaster relief efforts, or social justice initiatives, emphasizing the common human desire to make a positive impact.

**Emphasizing Reason:** While religious participants in interfaith dialogue may draw on faith-based reasoning, atheists often emphasize reason and evidence-based thinking in their contributions to discussions.

So atheists engage in interfaith dialogue with a focus on secularism, human-centered values and ethical collaboration. They seek to promote understanding, build bridges, address prejudice and advocate for a society that respects the freedom of belief and non-belief. Interfaith dialogue provides a platform for atheists to participate in discussions that transcend religious boundaries and promote a more inclusive and harmonious world.

# Chapter 39: Atheist Responses to Mystical Experiences

Mystical experiences, characterized by a profound sense of unity, transcendence, or connection with something greater than oneself, have been reported by individuals across different cultures and belief systems. While mysticism is often associated with religious and spiritual contexts, atheists, who typically do not hold belief in deities or the supernatural, also encounter and respond to these experiences. Let's explore how atheists respond to mystical experiences and the naturalistic perspectives they bring to such encounters.

**Naturalistic Explanations:** Atheists approach mystical experiences from a naturalistic perspective, seeking explanations rooted in psychology, neuroscience and the workings of the human brain.

**Psychological Insights:** Many atheists turn to psychology to understand the psychological mechanisms that may underlie mystical experiences. They explore concepts like altered states of consciousness, meditation and the brain's capacity for transcendent experiences.

**Neuroscientific Inquiry:** Atheists engage in neuroscientific research to investigate the neural processes associated with mystical experiences. They seek to uncover how the brain generates the sensations of unity and transcendence reported in these encounters.

**Subjective Nature:** Atheists recognize that mystical experiences are inherently subjective, varying widely among individuals. They understand that these experiences can be influenced by cultural, psychological and even social factors.

**Emphasis on Natural Causes:** Atheists emphasize that mystical experiences can have natural causes and do not necessarily point to the existence of supernatural entities or realms. They encourage critical inquiry into the origins of such experiences.

**Exploration of Consciousness:** Some atheists view mystical experiences as a fascinating aspect of human consciousness. They explore these experiences as opportunities to better understand the workings of the human mind.

**Philosophical Inquiry:** Mystical experiences may prompt philosophical inquiry among atheists. They contemplate questions related to the nature of consciousness, the self and the boundaries of human perception.

**Transcendence Within Naturalism:** Atheists may find a sense of transcendence or wonder within the naturalistic framework. They appreciate the awe and beauty of the natural world as a source of inspiration and wonder.

**Mind-Body Connection:** Atheists often consider the mind-body connection when responding to mystical experiences. They explore how altered states of consciousness can be induced through practices like meditation, demonstrating the influence of mental states on perception.

**Empirical Exploration:** Atheists encourage empirical exploration of mystical experiences, using scientific methods to investigate their underlying mechanisms. They seek to demystify these encounters and shed light on their natural origins.

**Secular Spirituality:** Some atheists incorporate aspects of secular spirituality into their response to mystical experiences. They appreciate the sense of wonder and connection with the universe that can be derived from naturalistic perspectives.

So atheists respond to mystical experiences by seeking naturalistic explanations rooted in psychology, neuroscience and the subjective nature of these encounters. They explore the mind-body connection, emphasize the importance of empirical inquiry and may find a sense of awe and wonder within the naturalistic framework. Mystical experiences are seen as fascinating aspects of human consciousness to be understood through the lens of science and reason.

# Chapter 40: The Connection Between Atheism and Secular Humanism

Atheism and secular humanism are two distinct but closely related worldviews that share common principles and values. Let's explore the connection between atheism and secular humanism, examining how they overlap and how they differ in their philosophical foundations and goals.

**Atheism Defined:** Atheism is, at its core, the disbelief in deities or gods. It is a position that lacks a belief in supernatural entities and often relies on reason, skepticism and evidence-based thinking to guide one's understanding of the world.

**Secular Humanism Defined:** Secular humanism is a comprehensive worldview that places human values, ethics and well-being at its center. It embraces reason, ethics and compassion while rejecting supernatural beliefs and divine authority.

***Overlapping Values:***

**Naturalism:** Both atheism and secular humanism are grounded in naturalistic perspectives, emphasizing the importance of the natural world and rejecting supernatural explanations.

**Reason:** Both worldviews prioritize reason, critical thinking and evidence-based decision-making as essential tools for understanding the world and making ethical choices.

**Ethics:** Ethics play a central role in both atheism and secular humanism. They emphasize the importance of ethical principles rooted in empathy, compassion and the well-being of individuals and society.

**Secularism:** Both atheism and secular humanism advocate for secularism, the separation of church and state and the importance of maintaining a secular government that does not favor any particular religion.

***Key Differences:***

**Scope:** Atheism is primarily concerned with the question of belief in gods or deities, whereas secular humanism is a broader worldview that encompasses a wide range of human values, including ethics, morality and social justice.

**Positive Values:** While atheism is a position that negates belief in gods, secular humanism is a positive and proactive worldview that promotes human flourishing, well-being and the pursuit of ethical values.

**Social Justice:** Secular humanism often places a strong emphasis on social justice and the promotion of equitable and inclusive societies, advocating for equal rights, justice and human dignity for all individuals, regardless of their beliefs.

**Community:** Secular humanism often involves the building of communities and organizations that promote secular values, ethics and social goals. Atheism, as a singular position, may or may not involve active community engagement.

### *Complementary Perspectives:*

Atheism and secular humanism are complementary perspectives. Atheism provides a foundational stance on the existence of deities, while secular humanism offers a comprehensive ethical framework for guiding human behavior and decision-making.

Many atheists embrace secular humanist principles, seeing them as a natural extension of their rejection of religious beliefs. They appreciate the positive, human-centered values that secular humanism promotes.

### *Shared Goals:*

Both atheism and secular humanism share common goals, such as promoting reason, ethics, secularism and the well-being of humanity.

They often collaborate on social and political issues related to church-state separation, human rights, scientific literacy and social justice.

So atheism and secular humanism share common values such as naturalism, reason, ethics and secularism. While atheism is primarily a position on the existence of deities, secular humanism is a comprehensive worldview that promotes human well-being, social justice and ethical values. They are interconnected perspectives that often work together to advocate for a more rational, ethical and inclusive world.

# Chapter 41: Atheism and the Pursuit of Wisdom

Wisdom, often defined as the ability to apply knowledge and experience to make sound judgments and decisions, is a universal human aspiration that transcends religious and non-religious worldviews. Atheists, who typically ground their beliefs in reason, evidence and the natural world, also pursue wisdom, albeit from a secular and humanistic perspective. Let's explore how atheists approach the pursuit of wisdom and the values they uphold in their quest for understanding and insight.

**Reason as a Guiding Principle:** Atheists place a strong emphasis on reason and critical thinking in their pursuit of wisdom. They believe that sound judgment and decision-making are best achieved through rational inquiry and evidence-based analysis.

**Empirical Inquiry:** Many atheists value empirical inquiry as a means of gaining knowledge and wisdom. They emphasize the importance of observation, experimentation and the scientific method in understanding the natural world and human behavior.

**Ethical Considerations:** Wisdom for atheists often includes ethical considerations. They believe that true wisdom encompasses not only knowledge but also the ability to make ethical choices that promote the well-being of individuals and society.

**Human-Centered Values:** Atheists pursue wisdom with human-centered values in mind, such as empathy, compassion and justice. They see wisdom as a tool for enhancing the quality of life for themselves and others.

**Philosophical Exploration:** Atheists engage in philosophical exploration as part of their pursuit of wisdom. They contemplate questions related to existence, morality, meaning and the nature of reality, seeking insights that can inform their worldview.

**Lifelong Learning:** Wisdom is seen as a lifelong journey for atheists. They embrace the idea that there is always more to learn and understand and they remain open to new ideas and perspectives.

**Skepticism and Critical Thinking:** Skepticism and critical thinking are key tools in the atheist's pursuit of wisdom. They question assumptions, challenge beliefs and seek to discern between reliable information and unfounded claims.

**Community and Collaboration:** Atheists often collaborate with others in their pursuit of wisdom. They value the exchange of ideas, discussions and debates as ways to refine their thinking and gain new insights.

**Cultural and Historical Perspectives:** Wisdom for atheists includes an appreciation of cultural and historical perspectives. They study the wisdom traditions of various cultures and eras, recognizing the richness of human thought throughout history.

**Secular Ethics:** Wisdom often involves the application of secular ethics for atheists. They seek to make ethical decisions that align with humanistic values and principles, promoting fairness, equality and the well-being of all.

**Practical Wisdom:** Practical wisdom, or the ability to make sound decisions in real-life situations, is a central focus for atheists. They strive to apply their knowledge and understanding to navigate life's challenges effectively.

**Moral Responsibility:** Wisdom carries with it a sense of moral responsibility for atheists. They believe that as rational beings, they have a duty to make ethical choices that contribute positively to the betterment of society.

So atheists pursue wisdom with a strong emphasis on reason, empirical inquiry, ethical considerations and human-centered values. They engage in philosophical exploration, embrace lifelong learning and apply critical thinking in their quest for understanding and insight. Wisdom, for atheists, is a means of enhancing both individual and collective well-being while upholding the principles of reason and secular ethics.

# Chapter 42: Ethics Without Religion

Ethics, the study of moral principles and values that guide human behavior, has been a fundamental aspect of human societies for millennia. While many ethical systems have been influenced by religious beliefs, atheists demonstrate that a robust and meaningful ethical framework can exist independently of religion. Let's explore the concept of ethics without religion and how atheists approach moral decision-making.

**Secular Ethics Defined:** Secular ethics, also known as non-religious ethics or moral secularism, is an approach to ethics that does not rely on religious doctrines or divine authority to determine right and wrong. Instead, it derives moral principles from secular sources, such as reason, empathy, social consensus and human well-being.

**Human-Centered Values:** Secular ethics often places human well-being and flourishing at its core. Atheists emphasize that ethical decisions should prioritize the welfare and happiness of individuals and society.

**Reason-Based Morality:** Atheists assert that moral principles can be derived through reason and critical thinking. They believe that ethical decisions should be based on evidence, rational inquiry and ethical considerations that align with human values.

**Empathy and Compassion:** Empathy and compassion play a central role in secular ethics. Atheists emphasize the importance of understanding and caring for the experiences and well-being of others.

**Ethical Relativism:** Secular ethics acknowledges that ethical standards can vary across cultures and contexts. It encourages individuals to consider cultural, societal and situational factors when making moral judgments.

**Social Consensus:** Atheists often look to social consensus and human rights as sources of ethical guidance. They believe that ethical principles should be grounded in principles that promote fairness, equality and justice.

**Moral Dilemmas:** Atheists recognize that ethical decision-making can involve complex moral dilemmas. They engage in ethical discussions and debates to explore and resolve such dilemmas through reasoned discourse.

**Human Rights:** Secular ethics frequently align with principles of human rights. Atheists advocate for the protection of individual rights and freedoms, regardless of one's religious beliefs or non-belief.

**Secular Humanism:** Many atheists embrace secular humanism, a worldview that combines secular ethics with humanistic values. Secular humanism emphasizes the importance of reason, ethics and the well-being of humanity.

**Ethical Application:** Atheists apply secular ethics to various aspects of life, including personal relationships, societal issues and public policy. They seek to make ethical choices that promote a more just and compassionate world.

**Critique of Divine Command Theory:** Atheists often critique divine command theory, the ethical view that actions are morally right simply because they are commanded by a deity. They argue that this view can lead to moral relativism and a lack of accountability.

**Ethical Development:** Secular ethics emphasizes the development of ethical principles and personal growth. Atheists view ethical decision-making as a continuous process that involves self-reflection and moral improvement.

So ethics without religion, or secular ethics, is a robust and rational approach to moral decision-making embraced by atheists. It emphasizes human-centered values, reason-based morality, empathy and ethical principles that promote the well-being of individuals and society. While it stands independent of religious beliefs, secular ethics provides a meaningful and principled foundation for ethical decision-making in the absence of divine authority.

# Chapter 43: Atheist Contemplation of the Cosmos

The vast expanse of the cosmos, with its billions of galaxies, stars and planets, has long captivated human imagination and curiosity. Atheists, who often approach the world through a naturalistic and evidence-based lens, also engage in contemplation of the cosmos. Let's explore how atheists contemplate the universe, its mysteries and the naturalistic perspectives they bring to the cosmic wonders that surround us.

**Naturalistic Wonder:** Atheists often find wonder and awe in the natural world, including the cosmos. They see the universe as a source of inspiration and beauty, appreciating its intricacy and grandeur from a naturalistic standpoint.

**Scientific Inquiry:** Contemplation of the cosmos for atheists often involves scientific inquiry. They engage with fields like astronomy, astrophysics and cosmology to gain a deeper understanding of the universe's origins, structure and evolution.

**Cosmic Evolution:** Atheists embrace the scientific understanding of cosmic evolution, which explains the formation of galaxies, stars and planets over billions of years. They marvel at the processes that have shaped the cosmos without resorting to supernatural explanations.

**Sense of Scale:** Contemplating the cosmos allows atheists to gain a sense of the vast scale of the universe. They appreciate the humbling realization that Earth is but a tiny speck in a vast cosmic arena.

**Origins and Origins Questions:** Atheists explore questions related to the origins of the universe, the conditions that led to the formation of galaxies and the emergence of life on Earth. They seek naturalistic explanations for these phenomena.

**Existential Reflection:** Contemplation of the cosmos can prompt existential reflection among atheists. They contemplate questions about the nature of existence, the human role in the universe and the potential for life beyond Earth.

**Scientific Discovery:** Atheists celebrate scientific discoveries related to the cosmos, from the detection of exoplanets to the study of cosmic microwave background radiation. They view these discoveries as achievements of human reason and curiosity.

**Appreciation for Astronomy:** Many atheists have a deep appreciation for astronomy and stargazing. They enjoy observing celestial phenomena like eclipses, meteor showers and the beauty of the night sky.

**Cosmic Time and Scale:** Contemplating the cosmos often involves thinking about cosmic time scales. Atheists are fascinated by the idea that the universe has existed for billions of years, with events unfolding over vast stretches of time.

**Exploration of Cosmic Mysteries:** The universe is full of mysteries, from the nature of dark matter and dark energy to the possibility of extraterrestrial life. Atheists engage in scientific and philosophical discussions to explore these enigmas.

**Inspiration for Human Endeavor:** Atheists are inspired by the cosmos in their pursuit of scientific knowledge and human achievement. They see the universe as a source of motivation for space exploration and scientific discovery.

So contemplation of the cosmos is a source of wonder, inspiration and scientific inquiry for atheists. They approach the universe with a naturalistic perspective, celebrating the beauty and complexity of the cosmos while seeking to unravel its mysteries through evidence-based exploration. The contemplation of the cosmos represents a profound and awe-inspiring aspect of the natural world for atheists.

# Chapter 44: Atheist Perspectives on Self-Identity

Self-identity, the complex and multifaceted concept of who we are as individuals, is a subject of deep exploration and contemplation for people of various beliefs, including atheists. Let's delve into how atheists approach self-identity, the factors that shape their sense of self and the philosophical and psychological perspectives they bring to this fundamental aspect of human existence.

**Naturalistic Framework:** Atheists often approach self-identity from a naturalistic framework, emphasizing that our identities are a product of our biology, experiences and the natural world. They view the self as a construct that arises from these natural processes.

**No Supernatural Self:** Atheists reject the idea of a supernatural or divine self that exists independently of the physical and psychological aspects of human existence. They see no evidence for the existence of a soul or transcendent self.

**Psychological Factors:** Atheists recognize the role of psychology in shaping self-identity. They explore how cognitive processes, emotions, memories and perceptions contribute to their sense of self.

**Biological Basis:** Atheists acknowledge the biological basis of self-identity, understanding that the brain plays a central role in generating our thoughts, emotions and self-awareness. They appreciate the intricacies of neuroscience in explaining aspects of identity.

**Narrative and Life Story:** Many atheists see self-identity as a narrative or life story. They believe that our sense of self is constructed through the stories we tell ourselves about our past, present and future, as well as our roles in society.

**Social Identity:** Atheists recognize the significance of social identity, understanding that our sense of self is influenced by the groups we belong to, our cultural background and the roles we assume in our communities.

**Individual Autonomy:** Atheists often emphasize individual autonomy and self-determination in shaping one's self-identity. They believe that individuals have the capacity to define themselves on their terms.

**Psychological Exploration:** Self-identity is a subject of psychological exploration for atheists. They engage in self-reflection, introspection and psychological inquiry to better understand their beliefs, values and personal growth.

**Ethical Considerations:** Atheists may consider ethical dimensions of self-identity, exploring questions related to personal values, moral development and the impact of their identity on their interactions with others.

**Continual Evolution:** Atheists often view self-identity as a dynamic and continually evolving aspect of life. They understand that personal growth and change are natural parts of the human experience.

**Existential Reflection:** Contemplating self-identity can prompt existential reflection among atheists. They contemplate questions related to the meaning and purpose of life, the nature of existence and the impact of their identity on their worldview.

**Human Connection:** Atheists recognize the importance of human connection and relationships in shaping self-identity. They value social interactions and the exchange of ideas as sources of personal growth and self-discovery.

So atheists approach self-identity from a naturalistic and psychological perspective, emphasizing the role of biology, experiences and social factors in shaping who they are. They see self-identity as a dynamic and evolving aspect of life, open to exploration and personal growth. While rejecting the notion of a supernatural self, atheists engage in introspection and contemplation to better understand their place in the natural world and their connections with others.

# Chapter 45: Atheist Views on Free Will

The concept of free will, the ability to make choices and decisions independently of external influences, has been a subject of philosophical debate for centuries. Atheists, who often approach questions of existence and morality from a naturalistic and evidence-based standpoint, also have diverse views on the topic of free will. Let's explore various atheist perspectives on free will and how these perspectives intersect with their broader worldviews.

**Determinism and Naturalism:** Many atheists align with determinism, the belief that all events, including human actions and choices, are the result of prior causes. They see the universe as governed by natural laws and physical processes, making free will an illusion.

**Compatibilism:** Some atheists embrace compatibilism, a perspective that reconciles free will with determinism. They argue that while our choices may be influenced by external factors, we can still have a form of free will within those constraints. Compatibilists often focus on the capacity for rational decision-making and personal autonomy.

**Hard Determinism:** Other atheists lean towards hard determinism, which posits that free will is entirely incompatible with determinism. They argue that if the universe operates according to fixed laws and causal chains, true free will cannot exist.

**Neuroscience and Cognitive Science:** Many atheists look to neuroscience and cognitive science for insights into the nature of free will. They consider research on brain processes and decision-making to be valuable in understanding the mechanisms behind human choices.

**Moral Responsibility:** Atheists who embrace determinism may grapple with questions of moral responsibility. They explore how moral judgments and ethical systems can be constructed in a deterministic framework, even if free will is considered an illusion.

**Ethical Implications:** Atheists often consider the ethical implications of their views on free will. Some argue that a deterministic worldview challenges traditional notions of blame and punishment, promoting a more compassionate and rehabilitative approach to justice.

**Existentialism:** Existentialist atheists, influenced by philosophers like Jean-Paul Sartre, emphasize individual responsibility and the creation of meaning in a seemingly indifferent universe. They may advocate for a form of free will that arises from the choices individuals make in defining their own existence.

**Debate and Exploration:** Atheists engage in ongoing debates and explorations of free will, recognizing that the topic is complex and multifaceted. They appreciate the philosophical depth that free will discussions bring to their worldview.

**Variety of Perspectives:** It's important to note that there is no single "atheist view" on free will. Atheists hold diverse beliefs on this topic, ranging from hard determinism to various forms of compatibilism and existentialism.

So atheist perspectives on free will are diverse and reflect a range of philosophical stances, from determinism to compatibilism and existentialism. While there is no uniform view within atheism, atheists approach the question of free will with an emphasis on naturalistic explanations and rational inquiry, often engaging in ethical and philosophical discussions about the implications of their beliefs.

# Chapter 46: Atheism and the Power of Storytelling

Storytelling has been a fundamental aspect of human culture and communication throughout history, transcending religious and non-religious worldviews. Atheists, who often approach life from a secular and naturalistic perspective, also recognize and harness the power of storytelling. Let's explore how storytelling intersects with atheism, the narratives atheists create and the impact of these stories on their worldview and advocacy.

**Personal Narratives:** Many atheists have personal narratives that recount their journeys from religious belief to atheism. These narratives often involve critical questioning, intellectual exploration and the rejection of supernatural beliefs.

**Identity Narratives:** Atheists may construct identity narratives that emphasize their secular humanist values, commitment to reason and evidence and their place in a diverse and inclusive global community.

**Morality and Ethics:** Storytelling can be a powerful tool for atheists to convey their moral and ethical values. They may use narratives to illustrate how secular humanism guides their decision-making and commitment to ethical principles.

**Challenging Religious Narratives:** Some atheists use storytelling to challenge religious narratives and dogmas. They may present alternative perspectives and narratives that promote secularism, skepticism and critical thinking.

**Promotion of Science and Reason:** Atheists often employ storytelling to promote the values of science, reason and skepticism. They may tell stories of scientific discoveries, the importance of evidence-based thinking and the wonders of the natural world.

**Community Building:** Storytelling plays a role in building atheist communities. Personal stories of coming out as atheists, facing societal challenges and finding supportive communities can inspire and connect individuals.

**Humanism and Compassion:** Atheists may use storytelling to highlight humanistic values, such as empathy, compassion and social justice. They share narratives that emphasize the importance of improving the well-being of humanity.

**Celebrating Life and Existence:** Atheists often use storytelling to celebrate life and existence in a naturalistic context. They may share narratives that find wonder and beauty in the cosmos, the diversity of life on Earth and the potential for human progress.

**Exploration of Meaning:** Storytelling provides atheists with a platform to explore questions of meaning and purpose in a world without divine guidance. They may craft narratives that showcase the human capacity to create meaning through relationships, achievements and personal growth.

**Advocacy and Activism:** Storytelling is a powerful tool for atheist advocacy and activism. It allows atheists to share their perspectives, challenge discrimination and promote secularism and the separation of church and state.

**Diversity of Voices:** The atheist community comprises a diverse range of voices and experiences. Storytelling reflects this diversity, with narratives that explore the intersections of atheism with various identities, cultures and backgrounds.

So storytelling is a dynamic and versatile aspect of atheist expression. It serves as a means of personal exploration, community building, advocacy and the promotion of secular humanism. Atheists use storytelling to convey their values, challenge religious narratives and celebrate the human experience in a naturalistic context. Through narratives, they engage with the world and share their perspectives on life, morality and existence.

# Chapter 47: The Importance of Empathy

Empathy, the ability to understand and share the feelings of others, is a fundamental aspect of human social interaction and morality. While empathy is not inherently tied to any particular belief system, atheists, like individuals from all walks of life, recognize the profound importance of empathy in shaping their values, relationships and contributions to a more compassionate world. Let's explore the significance of empathy and how it intersects with atheism and secular humanism.

**Empathy as a Human Trait:** Empathy is often viewed as a universal human trait, transcending religious and non-religious worldviews. It's an innate ability that allows individuals to connect with and understand the experiences of others.

**Moral Compass:** Empathy serves as a moral compass for many atheists. It guides their ethical decision-making by encouraging kindness, compassion and consideration for the well-being of others.

**Basis for Human Rights:** Empathy underpins the concept of human rights. Atheists, often advocates for secularism and humanism, believe that every individual deserves dignity, respect and equal treatment, grounded in empathy for their shared humanity.

**Ethical Behavior:** Empathy motivates atheists to engage in ethical behavior, both in their personal lives and as members of society. It encourages them to act in ways that alleviate suffering and promote the welfare of others.

**Social Cohesion:** Empathy fosters social cohesion and community building. Atheists recognize the importance of empathetic connections in forming supportive communities and fostering a sense of belonging.

**Interfaith and Interbelief Dialogue:** Empathy plays a role in interfaith and interbelief dialogue. Atheists engage with people of various belief systems, seeking to understand their perspectives and promoting respectful conversations based on empathy.

**Compassion for All:** Atheists often extend their empathy to all living beings, not just humans. They advocate for animal welfare and environmental conservation as expressions of their compassion for the broader natural world.

**Mitigating Prejudice:** Empathy helps atheists confront and mitigate prejudice and discrimination. They work to challenge biases and promote inclusivity, recognizing the importance of empathy in breaking down barriers.

**Conflict Resolution:** Empathy is a valuable tool in conflict resolution. Atheists strive to understand differing viewpoints and work toward peaceful solutions, acknowledging the role of empathy in resolving disputes.

**Promotion of Secular Humanism:** Empathy aligns with the principles of secular humanism, which emphasize the value and dignity of every individual. Atheists promote these values as they advocate for secularism and social justice.

**Cultivation of Empathy:** Atheists recognize that empathy can be cultivated and strengthened through education and practice. They engage in efforts to promote empathy in themselves and in society as a whole.

So empathy is a cornerstone of human morality and social interaction, recognized and embraced by atheists as a vital element of their worldview. Empathy informs their ethical decisions, relationships and advocacy for a more compassionate and inclusive world. While atheism itself is a disbelief in gods or deities, atheists frequently emphasize the importance of empathy in shaping their values and guiding their actions as secular humanists.

# Chapter 48: Atheism and the Challenge of Suffering

Suffering, in its many forms, is a deeply human experience that has long been a central concern in philosophical and religious discourse. Atheists, who disbelieve in divine or supernatural explanations for suffering, grapple with this existential challenge from a naturalistic perspective. Let's explore how atheism approaches the problem of suffering, the philosophical questions it raises and the strategies atheists employ to find meaning and address this universal human dilemma.

**Naturalistic Perspective:** Atheism begins with a naturalistic worldview, which means that atheists do not attribute suffering to supernatural causes or divine plans. They seek natural explanations for the causes of suffering.

**Empathy and Compassion:** Atheists often approach suffering with empathy and compassion, emphasizing the importance of alleviating the pain and distress of others. They view these values as intrinsic to humanism.

**The Existential Challenge:** The existence of suffering poses an existential challenge for atheists. It prompts questions about the nature of life, the human condition and the absence of cosmic meaning.

**Ethical Response:** Atheists believe in taking ethical responsibility for addressing suffering in the world. They advocate for social justice, humanitarian efforts and policies that reduce human suffering.

**Secular Support Systems:** Atheists recognize the value of secular support systems, including healthcare, social services and community networks, in addressing suffering and providing assistance to those in need.

**Embracing Empirical Evidence:** Atheists emphasize the importance of empirical evidence in understanding and addressing suffering. They support scientific research and evidence-based approaches to healthcare and social policy.

**Philosophical Exploration:** Suffering raises profound philosophical questions for atheists. They engage in philosophical inquiry to explore the nature of suffering, its causes and how humans can find meaning in a world without divine purpose.

**Human Resilience:** Atheists often celebrate human resilience in the face of suffering. They draw inspiration from stories of individuals who overcome adversity through courage, determination and community support.

**Existentialism and Meaning:** Some atheists draw from existentialist philosophy to find meaning in a world where suffering exists. They believe that individuals can create their own meaning through their choices and actions.

**Promotion of Well-Being:** Atheists emphasize the promotion of well-being as a central goal in addressing suffering. They support initiatives that improve mental and physical health, reduce poverty and enhance quality of life.

**Championing Secular Ethics:** Atheists advocate for secular ethics that prioritize human welfare and minimize harm. They argue that ethical systems can be constructed without reliance on religious dogma.

**Continual Exploration:** The challenge of suffering remains an ongoing concern for atheists. They engage in continual exploration, dialogue and advocacy to address suffering and improve the human condition.

So atheists approach the challenge of suffering from a naturalistic and humanistic standpoint. They seek to alleviate human suffering through empathy, compassion, ethical action and the promotion of secular values. While acknowledging the existential questions raised by suffering, atheists emphasize the importance of evidence-based approaches to understanding and addressing this universal aspect of the human experience.

# Chapter 49: Atheist Approaches to Meditation Practices

Meditation, a practice that involves focused attention and mindfulness, has been embraced by individuals of various belief systems as a means to cultivate mental clarity, reduce stress and promote well-being. While meditation has strong ties to religious traditions, including Buddhism and Hinduism, it has also found a place among atheists and secular humanists. Let's explore how atheists approach meditation practices, the benefits they derive from them and the secular contexts in which meditation is employed.

**Secular Meditation:** Many atheists engage in secular forms of meditation that do not involve religious or spiritual beliefs. These practices emphasize the mental and physical benefits of meditation without invoking supernatural elements.

**Stress Reduction and Mental Health:** Atheists appreciate meditation for its ability to reduce stress and promote mental health. They view it as a valuable tool for managing the pressures of daily life.

**Cognitive Benefits:** Meditation is seen as a means to enhance cognitive functioning, including improved attention, memory and problem-solving skills. Atheists embrace these cognitive benefits in their secular practice.

**Emotional Regulation:** Atheists use meditation to improve emotional regulation and cultivate a greater sense of emotional well-being. It can help them manage anxiety, depression and other emotional challenges.

**Physical Health:** Meditation practices are recognized for their potential physical health benefits, such as reduced blood pressure and enhanced immune function. Atheists value these aspects of meditation for overall well-being.

**Scientific Approach:** Atheists often approach meditation from a scientific perspective, appreciating the extensive research on its effects. They seek evidence-based practices that align with a naturalistic worldview.

**Mind-Body Connection:** Meditation allows atheists to explore the mind-body connection without invoking spiritual beliefs. They appreciate the connection between mental and physical health.

**Atheistic Mindfulness:** Some atheists incorporate mindfulness into their daily lives, using it as a tool to stay focused, grounded and attentive to their surroundings.

**Community and Support:** Atheists may engage in group meditation sessions or classes as a means of building community and support networks. These secular meditation communities provide a sense of belonging.

**Personal Growth and Reflection:** Meditation practices encourage atheists to engage in personal growth and self-reflection. It allows them to explore their thoughts, values and aspirations in a secular context.

**Ethical Living:** For some atheists, meditation serves as a tool for ethical living. It helps them cultivate empathy, compassion and a deeper understanding of their own values and principles.

So atheists embrace meditation practices as valuable tools for enhancing mental and physical well-being, reducing stress and promoting mindfulness. They approach meditation from a secular and evidence-based perspective, appreciating the benefits it offers without invoking religious or supernatural beliefs. Meditation is seen as a practice that aligns with a naturalistic worldview and complements the principles of secular humanism.

# Chapter 50: Atheist Views on Altruism

Altruism, the selfless concern for the well-being of others, is a concept deeply ingrained in human morality and social behavior. While religious traditions often promote altruism as a virtue, atheists, who do not rely on religious teachings for their ethical framework, also value and embrace altruistic principles. Let's explore how atheists view and practice altruism, the motivations behind their altruistic actions and the role of empathy and humanism in shaping their approach to helping others.

**Human-Centered Altruism:** Atheists often view altruism as a human-centered virtue, rooted in empathy and compassion for fellow human beings. They believe in the intrinsic value of helping others, irrespective of religious beliefs.

**Empathy and Compassion:** Empathy and compassion play a central role in motivating atheists to engage in altruistic acts. They believe in the importance of alleviating suffering and promoting well-being as expressions of human empathy.

**Secular Ethics:** Altruism aligns with the secular ethics embraced by many atheists. They emphasize the need for ethical systems that promote human welfare, social justice and the betterment of society.

**Ethical Responsibility:** Atheists often see altruism as an ethical responsibility, grounded in a commitment to promoting the welfare of all individuals, regardless of their religious or non-religious beliefs.

**Community Support:** Atheists recognize the value of community support in times of need. They engage in altruistic actions to strengthen their communities and provide assistance to those facing adversity.

**Humanitarian Efforts:** Many atheists are involved in humanitarian efforts, including volunteering, charitable donations and advocacy for social causes. They seek to address pressing global issues, such as poverty, inequality and access to education and healthcare.

**Promotion of Secular Altruism:** Atheists advocate for secular altruism, emphasizing that altruistic actions do not require religious motivation. They promote a worldview in which humanistic values guide ethical behavior.

**Building Inclusive Communities:** Altruism is seen as a means of building inclusive and supportive communities. Atheists value the creation of spaces where individuals from diverse backgrounds can come together to help one another.

**Moral Principles:** Altruism is considered a fundamental moral principle by many atheists. They strive to align their actions with principles that prioritize the well-being and dignity of every individual.

**Empowerment Through Education:** Atheists often emphasize the role of education in empowering individuals to make informed and altruistic choices. They support educational initiatives that promote critical thinking and empathy.

**Global Perspective:** Atheists engage in altruistic actions on a global scale, recognizing that human welfare extends beyond borders and religious affiliations. They seek to address global challenges and promote a more compassionate world.

So atheists view and practice altruism as an essential aspect of human morality and social responsibility. They are motivated by empathy, compassion and humanistic values to engage in altruistic actions that promote the well-being of individuals and communities. Altruism is a reflection of their commitment to ethical principles that prioritize human welfare, irrespective of religious beliefs.

# Chapter 51: Atheist Reflections on Beauty

Beauty is a concept that has intrigued and inspired humans throughout history. While religious and spiritual traditions often attribute beauty to divine creation, atheists approach beauty from a naturalistic and humanistic perspective. Let's explore how atheists reflect on and appreciate beauty, both in the natural world and in human creativity and how their worldview shapes their perceptions of the beautiful.

**Natural Beauty:** Many atheists find profound beauty in the natural world. They are inspired by the awe-inspiring landscapes, intricate ecosystems and the wonders of the cosmos. For atheists, the beauty of nature is a testament to the power of natural processes.

**Science and Beauty:** Atheists often appreciate the beauty in scientific discoveries. They see elegance and wonder in the laws of physics, the complexity of biological systems and the mysteries of the universe. Scientific exploration itself is seen as a pursuit of beauty in understanding.

**Human Creativity:** Atheists recognize the beauty in human creativity, including art, music, literature and architecture. They celebrate the capacity of humans to express themselves and create works that evoke deep emotions.

**Ethical Beauty:** For some atheists, beauty is intertwined with ethics. They find beauty in acts of kindness, compassion and social justice. The pursuit of a more equitable and compassionate world is seen as a beautiful endeavor.

**Aesthetic Experience:** Atheists value the aesthetic experience, which includes moments of intense beauty and appreciation. These experiences may arise from encounters with art, music, nature, or acts of human kindness.

**Subjective Nature of Beauty:** Atheists often recognize that beauty is subjective. What one person finds beautiful, another may not. This subjectivity encourages a diversity of perspectives and interpretations of beauty.

**Artistic Expression:** Many atheists engage in artistic expression as a means of exploring and sharing their perceptions of beauty. They use art to convey their naturalistic and humanistic worldview.

**Human Connection:** Beauty can foster a sense of connection among atheists. They appreciate the shared experience of beauty and the conversations it can spark about the natural world, creativity and the human condition.

**Awe and Wonder:** Atheists experience awe and wonder in the absence of supernatural explanations. They find wonder in the mysteries of the universe and the intricacies of life on Earth.

**Continual Exploration:** Atheists approach beauty with a sense of continual exploration. They seek to discover new sources of beauty, whether in scientific discoveries, artistic expressions, or moments of everyday life.

So atheists reflect on and appreciate beauty in diverse ways, finding it in the natural world, human creativity, ethical actions and the subjective experiences of awe and wonder. Their naturalistic and humanistic worldview encourages a deep appreciation for the beauty that exists within and beyond the human experience.

# Chapter 52: Atheism and the Philosophy of Happiness

Happiness is a fundamental pursuit for humans across cultures and belief systems. While religious traditions often provide specific guidelines for attaining happiness, atheists approach this pursuit from a secular and philosophical standpoint. Let's explore how atheists contemplate and seek happiness, the philosophical underpinnings of their perspective and the factors that contribute to their sense of well-being.

**Secular Pursuit of Happiness:** Atheists pursue happiness without relying on religious or supernatural beliefs. They seek to lead fulfilling lives based on naturalistic and humanistic principles.

**Ethical Foundations:** Happiness for atheists is often grounded in ethical principles, such as compassion, empathy and social justice. They believe that a just and equitable society is essential for individual and collective well-being.

**Human Flourishing:** Many atheists define happiness as a component of human flourishing. They view well-being as encompassing physical, mental and emotional health, as well as personal growth and a sense of purpose.

**Rationality and Critical Thinking:** Atheists value rationality and critical thinking as tools for achieving happiness. They seek evidence-based strategies for making informed decisions and solving problems.

**Positive Psychology:** Positive psychology, a field that studies the science of well-being and happiness, aligns with atheistic principles. Atheists may draw from this discipline to enhance their happiness and life satisfaction.

**Personal Growth and Fulfillment:** Atheists often find happiness in personal growth, self-discovery and the pursuit of meaningful goals.

They view life as an opportunity for self-improvement and self-fulfillment.

**Secular Morality and Altruism:** Happiness is linked to secular morality and altruism for atheists. They derive satisfaction from helping others and promoting a more compassionate and just society.

**Intrinsic Value of Life:** Atheists often emphasize the intrinsic value of life and the preciousness of the here and now. They find happiness in the moments and experiences that life offers.

**Community and Connection:** Happiness is closely tied to community and connection for atheists. They value relationships with like-minded individuals who share their secular values and goals.

**Philosophical Exploration:** Atheists engage in philosophical exploration to understand the nature of happiness and the meaning of life. They may draw from secular philosophies that promote human flourishing.

**Promotion of Happiness:** Atheists often advocate for policies and social systems that promote happiness and well-being on a societal level. They believe that the pursuit of happiness should be accessible to all.

So atheists pursue happiness from a secular and humanistic perspective, grounded in ethical principles, rationality and a commitment to individual and collective well-being. They find happiness in personal growth, community, connection and the intrinsic value of life. Atheism encourages a thoughtful and evidence-based approach to the pursuit of happiness, fostering a sense of purpose and contentment in the absence of religious beliefs.

# Chapter 53: Atheist Perspectives on Healing and Wellness

Healing and wellness are universal human concerns that extend beyond religious beliefs. Atheists approach these aspects of life from a secular standpoint, emphasizing naturalistic explanations and evidence-based practices. Let's explore how atheists view healing and wellness, the importance they place on science and medicine and their holistic approach to well-being.

**Naturalistic Healing:** Atheists approach healing with a naturalistic worldview, seeking natural explanations for physical and mental health conditions. They do not attribute illness to supernatural causes.

**Science and Medicine:** Central to atheist perspectives on healing is a strong reliance on science and evidence-based medicine. They value medical research, healthcare and scientific advancements in improving human health.

**Preventative Care:** Atheists recognize the value of preventative care in maintaining good health. They emphasize healthy lifestyle choices, regular check-ups and vaccinations as crucial aspects of well-being.

**Mental Health and Psychology:** Atheists acknowledge the importance of mental health and psychology in overall wellness. They view mental health as an integral part of a person's well-being and support evidence-based approaches to mental health care.

**Holistic Approach:** Atheists often take a holistic approach to wellness, considering physical, mental and emotional well-being as interconnected. They promote practices that support overall health and balance.

**Healthy Skepticism:** Atheists maintain a healthy skepticism toward alternative and unproven healing practices. They prioritize treatments with a strong scientific foundation and are cautious about pseudoscientific or faith-based claims.

**Community Support:** Atheists may seek support within their secular communities when facing health challenges. They recognize the value of emotional and practical support from like-minded individuals.

**Bioethics and Medical Ethics:** Ethics play a significant role in atheist perspectives on healing and wellness. They engage in discussions about bioethics and medical ethics, particularly in areas such as end-of-life decisions and reproductive rights.

**Access to Healthcare:** Many atheists advocate for universal access to healthcare as a fundamental human right. They believe that healthcare should be accessible to all, regardless of religious or non-religious beliefs.

**Wellness Promotion:** Atheists actively promote wellness in their communities. They may organize events or initiatives that focus on healthy living, mental health awareness and wellness education.

**Lifespan Considerations:** Atheists may reflect on the human lifespan and the importance of making the most of the time one has. They emphasize living a meaningful and fulfilling life, focusing on well-being at all stages.

**Ethical Willingness:** In situations where medical decisions are required, atheists often express their wishes in advance through ethical wills or advance directives. They ensure that their healthcare decisions align with their secular values.

So atheists approach healing and wellness from a naturalistic and evidence-based perspective, valuing science, medicine and preventative care. They prioritize overall well-being, including physical and mental health and advocate for universal access to healthcare. Atheist perspectives on healing and wellness reflect a commitment to rationality, ethics and a holistic approach to human flourishing.

# Chapter 54: The Intersection of Atheism and Social Activism

Atheism, as the disbelief in deities, is often viewed as a singular aspect of an individual's worldview. However, for many atheists, this lack of religious belief intersects with their commitment to social activism and humanistic values. Let's explore how atheism and social activism intersect, the issues that motivate atheist activists and the ways they contribute to positive social change.

**Secular Humanism:** Many atheists embrace secular humanism, a worldview that places a strong emphasis on reason, ethics and the promotion of human welfare. This humanistic philosophy often underpins their commitment to social activism.

**Advocacy for Secularism:** Atheist activists often advocate for the separation of church and state, ensuring that religious beliefs do not unduly influence government policies and public institutions.

**Religious Freedom and Equality:** Atheists champion religious freedom and equality, advocating for the right of individuals to hold diverse religious or non-religious beliefs without facing discrimination.

**Social Justice:** Many atheists are passionate about social justice issues, including gender equality, LGBTQ+ rights, racial justice, economic inequality and access to education and healthcare.

**Science and Education:** Atheist activists promote science, critical thinking and evidence-based education. They advocate for the inclusion of scientific principles in public policy and the curriculum.

**Secular Morality:** Social activism among atheists is often motivated by secular moral principles. They emphasize the importance of ethical behavior, compassion and empathy as guiding values.

**Political Engagement:** Atheists engage in political activism to promote secular values and advocate for policies that align with their principles. They support candidates who prioritize evidence-based decision-making.

**Community Building:** Atheist communities often play a role in social activism. They provide a platform for like-minded individuals to organize and mobilize for various causes.

**Global Initiatives:** Atheist activists may engage in global initiatives to address issues like religious persecution, blasphemy laws and the promotion of secular values worldwide.

**Interfaith and Interbelief Dialogue:** Some atheist organizations participate in interfaith and interbelief dialogue to foster understanding and cooperation among individuals with diverse worldviews. They seek common ground on shared values and goals.

**Legal Challenges:** Atheist groups may initiate or support legal challenges to practices that violate the principle of church-state separation. They work to ensure that public institutions remain neutral on matters of religion.

**Supporting Marginalized Communities:** Atheist activists often support marginalized and underrepresented communities, including secular individuals who may face discrimination or social isolation due to their non-religious beliefs.

So the intersection of atheism and social activism is marked by a commitment to secular humanism, ethical principles and a passion for social justice. Atheist activists advocate for a range of issues, from secularism and religious freedom to social equality and scientific literacy. Their activism reflects a dedication to evidence-based reasoning, compassion and the betterment of society, irrespective of religious beliefs.

# Chapter 55: Atheist Explorations of the Sublime

The sublime, a concept often associated with religious or spiritual experiences, has also captivated atheists who approach it from a secular and naturalistic perspective. Let's delve into how atheists explore and appreciate the sublime in various aspects of life, from the natural world to human creativity and how they derive a sense of wonder and awe without invoking the divine.

**Natural Wonders:** Atheists often find the sublime in the natural world. They are awed by the grandeur of mountains, the vastness of oceans, the intricacies of ecosystems and the mysteries of the cosmos.

**Scientific Discoveries:** Scientific revelations can evoke a sense of the sublime among atheists. They appreciate the beauty and wonder found in the laws of physics, the complexity of biology and the elegance of mathematics.

**Human Creativity:** Atheists explore the sublime in human creativity. They are moved by art, music, literature and architecture that evoke deep emotions and offer new perspectives on the human experience.

**Secular Spirituality:** Some atheists embrace a form of secular spirituality that allows them to explore the sublime in the here and now. They seek moments of transcendence and awe without invoking the supernatural.

**Cosmic Perspective:** The exploration of space and our place in the universe can inspire a sense of the sublime in atheists. They contemplate the vastness of the cosmos and our role as sentient beings in it.

**Moral and Ethical Beauty:** Atheists may find the sublime in acts of kindness, compassion and social justice. They appreciate the beauty of ethical behavior and the potential for humanity to make positive change.

**Interconnectedness:** Atheists explore the idea of interconnectedness in a naturalistic sense. They see beauty in the interconnected web of life on Earth and the relationships between all living beings.

**Philosophical Reflection:** Atheists engage in philosophical reflection to explore the sublime. They ponder questions about the nature of existence, the meaning of life and the mysteries of consciousness.

**Wonder and Awe:** Wonder and awe are often central to atheist explorations of the sublime. They seek moments of intense curiosity and appreciation for the world around them.

**Transcendence of Self:** Atheists may experience a form of transcendence through self-discovery and personal growth. They find the sublime in the realization of their own potential.

**Collective Experience:** Exploring the sublime can be a collective experience for atheists. They may share moments of wonder and awe with like-minded individuals who appreciate the naturalistic world.

So atheists explore and appreciate the sublime in various aspects of life, from the natural world to human creativity and ethical behavior. They seek moments of transcendence, wonder and awe within a secular and naturalistic framework, finding beauty and inspiration in the mysteries and complexities of existence. The sublime, for atheists, is a source of wonder and a testament to the richness of the natural world.

# Chapter 56: Atheism and the Art of Compassion

Compassion, often associated with religious teachings, is a value that extends beyond the boundaries of belief systems. Atheists, who do not hold religious or supernatural beliefs, also place great importance on compassion and empathy in their lives. Let's explore how atheists practice and embody compassion, the philosophical foundations of their compassionate worldview and the impact of their actions on individuals and communities.

**Secular Morality:** Compassion is a cornerstone of secular morality for atheists. They believe in the intrinsic value of empathy, kindness and altruism as guiding principles for ethical behavior.

**Empathy and Human Connection:** Atheists recognize the significance of empathy and human connection in fostering compassion. They empathize with the struggles and suffering of others and seek to alleviate it.

**Ethical Behavior:** Compassionate actions are closely aligned with ethical behavior for atheists. They prioritize actions that promote the well-being of individuals and communities, irrespective of religious beliefs.

**Social Justice and Equity:** Many atheists are passionate advocates for social justice and equity. They work to address issues such as gender equality, LGBTQ+ rights, racial justice, economic inequality and access to education and healthcare.

**Community Building:** Compassion often plays a central role in building secular communities. Atheists create spaces where like-minded individuals can support each other, offer help to those in need and collectively engage in acts of compassion.

**Altruistic Endeavors:** Atheists engage in altruistic endeavors, including volunteering, charitable donations and community service.

They find fulfillment in giving back to their communities and contributing to the greater good.

**Educational Initiatives:** Compassion drives many atheists to support educational initiatives that promote critical thinking, empathy and ethical reasoning. They believe that education is a pathway to a more compassionate society.

**Global Impact:** Atheists extend their compassion to global initiatives, advocating for humanitarian efforts, disaster relief and addressing global challenges, such as poverty, healthcare disparities and climate change.

**Interfaith and Interbelief Dialogue:** Some atheist organizations participate in interfaith and interbelief dialogue, fostering understanding and cooperation among individuals with diverse worldviews. They seek common ground on shared values, including compassion.

**Philosophical Reflection:** Atheists engage in philosophical reflection on the nature of compassion and its role in human existence. They contemplate questions related to empathy, altruism and the moral responsibility to alleviate suffering.

**Cultivating Compassion:** Compassion is considered a quality that can be cultivated and developed through self-reflection and acts of kindness. Atheists actively work to nurture their capacity for compassion.

So atheism and the art of compassion go hand in hand for many atheists. They prioritize compassion as a fundamental value, emphasizing empathy, ethical behavior and social justice. Their actions, both individually and collectively, reflect a commitment to making the world a more compassionate and equitable place, irrespective of religious beliefs.

# Chapter 57: Atheist Reflections on Diversity and Inclusion

Diversity and inclusion are important principles for atheists, who value pluralism, equity and the recognition of the dignity of every individual. Let's explore how atheists reflect on diversity and inclusion, their commitment to creating welcoming and inclusive communities and their advocacy for equal rights and opportunities for all, regardless of religious or non-religious beliefs.

**Pluralistic Communities:** Atheists often strive to create pluralistic communities that welcome individuals from diverse backgrounds, beliefs and identities.

**Equal Treatment and Respect:** Atheists emphasize the equal treatment and respect of all individuals, regardless of their religious or non-religious affiliations.

**LGBTQ+ Rights:** Many atheists are strong advocates for LGBTQ+ rights. They support equal marriage rights, nondiscrimination policies and the dismantling of harmful conversion therapies.

**Racial Justice:** Atheists recognize the importance of racial justice and equality. They support efforts to address systemic racism, promote diversity and combat racial discrimination.

**Gender Equality:** Gender equality is a central concern for atheists. They advocate for equal opportunities and rights for people of all genders.

**Religious Freedom:** While atheists may not hold religious beliefs themselves, they champion the principle of religious freedom. They believe that everyone has the right to practice their religion or non-religion without discrimination or persecution.

**Interfaith and Interbelief Dialogue:** Some atheist organizations engage in interfaith and interbelief dialogue to foster understanding and cooperation among individuals with diverse worldviews. They seek common ground on shared values, including inclusivity.

**Accessibility and Accommodation:** Atheists advocate for accessibility and accommodation in public spaces and institutions to ensure that individuals of all abilities can participate fully in society.

**Intersectionality:** Atheists recognize the importance of intersectionality, understanding that individuals may face multiple forms of discrimination or oppression simultaneously. They work to address these intersecting challenges.

**Educational Initiatives:** Atheists support educational initiatives that promote diversity, inclusion and tolerance. They seek to create a more informed and empathetic society.

**Secular Activism:** In their secular activism, atheists often emphasize the importance of a secular government that treats all citizens equally, regardless of their religious or non-religious beliefs.

**International Advocacy:** Atheists engage in international advocacy to support the rights of non-religious individuals and the promotion of secular values worldwide.

So atheists reflect on diversity and inclusion as core principles that align with their commitment to equal rights and opportunities for all. They advocate for the dismantling of discrimination, whether based on religious or non-religious beliefs and work toward creating inclusive communities and a more equitable society. Atheist reflections on diversity and inclusion emphasize the importance of recognizing the inherent worth and dignity of every individual, irrespective of their background or identity.

# Chapter 58: Atheist Perspectives on the Universe

Atheists approach the universe with a naturalistic and secular worldview, seeking to understand its origins, structure and mysteries through scientific inquiry and critical thinking. Let's delve into atheist perspectives on the universe, the scientific insights they embrace and their awe and wonder at the cosmos.

**Cosmic Origins:** Atheists accept the scientific consensus on the origins of the universe, which is explained by the Big Bang theory. They view the universe's emergence as a natural process.

**Natural Laws:** Atheists appreciate the elegance of the natural laws that govern the universe. They find beauty in the mathematical precision and predictability of physical phenomena.

**Absence of Cosmic Purpose:** Atheists reject the notion of a cosmic purpose or divine plan for the universe. They assert that meaning and purpose are human constructs, not inherent in the cosmos.

**Exploration of Space:** Many atheists are enthusiastic supporters of space exploration. They marvel at the achievements of human space exploration and the quest to understand the universe beyond Earth.

**The Scale of the Cosmos:** Atheists are humbled by the vastness of the cosmos. They contemplate the billions of galaxies, each containing billions of stars and the incomprehensible scale of the universe.

**Awe and Wonder:** Despite their naturalistic worldview, atheists experience awe and wonder when contemplating the universe's grandeur. They find inspiration in the mysteries yet to be unraveled.

**Scientific Exploration:** Atheists champion scientific exploration as the best tool for understanding the universe. They embrace the pursuit of knowledge and the importance of empirical evidence.

**Cosmic Evolution:** Atheists accept the scientific understanding of cosmic evolution, which explains the formation of galaxies, stars and planets over billions of years.

**Existential Reflection:** The contemplation of the universe often leads atheists to existential reflection. They ponder questions about their place in the cosmos and the significance of human existence.

**Atheism and Space Sciences:** Atheists often have a keen interest in space sciences, such as astrophysics, cosmology and astronomy. They appreciate the contributions of these fields to our understanding of the universe.

**Secular Cosmology:** Atheists embrace a secular cosmology that rejects supernatural explanations for the universe's origins and structure. They prioritize evidence-based understanding over mystical beliefs.

**The Search for Extraterrestrial Life:** Many atheists are intrigued by the search for extraterrestrial life. They see the discovery of life beyond Earth as a testament to the potential for life in the universe.

So atheists approach the universe with a sense of wonder, guided by scientific inquiry and a naturalistic worldview. They appreciate the elegance of natural laws, accept the scientific explanations for cosmic origins and find inspiration in the vastness and mysteries of the cosmos. While they reject the idea of a cosmic purpose, atheists embrace the pursuit of knowledge and the quest to understand the universe through empirical exploration.

# Chapter 59: The Role of Atheist Spirituality in Personal Fulfillment

Atheist spirituality may seem paradoxical, given that spirituality is often associated with religious beliefs. However, for many atheists, spirituality takes on a different form, one that doesn't rely on the supernatural but still plays a vital role in their personal fulfillment. Let's explore how atheist spirituality is defined, how it contributes to personal well-being and the practices and principles that atheists often embrace in their spiritual journeys.

**Defining Atheist Spirituality:** Atheist spirituality is a term used to describe the pursuit of inner peace, meaning and personal growth without relying on religious or supernatural beliefs. It's a form of secular spirituality.

**Values and Ethics:** For atheists, spirituality often revolves around a deep exploration of their values and ethics. They seek to live in alignment with their core principles, emphasizing empathy, reason and humanistic values.

**Connection to Nature:** Many atheists find spiritual connection in nature. They appreciate the beauty and wonder of the natural world and seek solace and inspiration in its presence.

**Human Connection:** Atheists value human connection and relationships as a source of spiritual fulfillment. They find meaning in their connections with others and the bonds they form.

**Transcendence through Art and Creativity:** Atheists often experience transcendence through art, music, writing and creative expression. These outlets allow them to tap into a sense of awe and wonder without resorting to supernatural explanations.

**Philosophical Reflection:** Atheist spirituality involves philosophical reflection on life's big questions, such as the nature of existence, the pursuit of meaning and the exploration of ethical principles.

**Awe and Wonder:** Awe and wonder are central to atheist spirituality. While they may not attribute these feelings to a divine source, atheists are captivated by the mysteries and beauty of the world.

**Personal Growth and Fulfillment:** The pursuit of personal growth and self-fulfillment is a key aspect of atheist spirituality. They strive to become the best versions of themselves and to lead meaningful lives.

**Social Engagement and Activism:** Atheists often find spiritual fulfillment in social engagement and activism. They seek to make a positive impact on society, driven by a sense of moral responsibility.

**Ethical Living:** Living ethically and making choices that align with their values is a form of spiritual practice for atheists. They believe that ethical living contributes to personal fulfillment.

**Secular Communities:** Atheist communities provide a space for spiritual exploration and fulfillment. These communities offer support, camaraderie and a sense of belonging.

So atheist spirituality is a deeply personal and meaningful pursuit that focuses on values, ethics, mindfulness and a sense of awe and wonder in the natural world. While it doesn't involve supernatural beliefs, it plays a significant role in personal fulfillment and the pursuit of a meaningful and purposeful life for many atheists.

# Chapter 60: Atheist Approaches to Overcoming Adversity

Life is filled with challenges and adversities and atheists, like anyone else, encounter difficult times. How atheists approach and overcome adversity often reflects their values, resilience and reliance on secular principles. Let's explore how atheists navigate life's challenges, find strength in their worldview and build strategies for resilience.

**Resilience through Reason:** Atheists often rely on reason and critical thinking to assess and address adversities. They approach problems methodically, seeking rational solutions.

**Community Support:** Atheist communities can provide crucial support during difficult times. These communities offer a sense of belonging, empathy and practical assistance.

**Psychological Resilience:** Atheists may draw on psychological resilience strategies, such as cognitive-behavioral techniques, mindfulness and emotional intelligence, to cope with adversity.

**Awe in Nature:** For some atheists, spending time in nature and appreciating its beauty can be a source of solace and rejuvenation during tough times.

**Secular Morality:** Atheists often derive strength from their secular moral values when facing adversity. They believe in acting ethically and with compassion, even in challenging circumstances.

**Human Connection:** Building and maintaining relationships is vital for atheists when dealing with adversity. They find solace and support in their connections with friends and loved ones.

**Acceptance and Stoicism:** Some atheists embrace principles of acceptance and stoicism, acknowledging that certain aspects of life are beyond their control and focusing on their responses to adversity.

**Problem-Solving:** Atheists are typically proactive in seeking solutions to problems. They analyze challenges, break them down into manageable steps and take action to address them.

**Advocacy and Activism:** Atheists may respond to adversity through advocacy and activism. They engage in efforts to address systemic issues, injustice, or discrimination.

**Humor and Coping:** Humor can be a coping mechanism for atheists during difficult times. They may use satire, irony, or comedy to navigate adversity and maintain a sense of perspective.

**Resilience through Knowledge:** Atheists often seek knowledge and information as a means to overcome adversity. They believe that understanding the root causes of problems can lead to effective solutions.

**Personal Growth:** Facing adversity can be an opportunity for personal growth for atheists. They strive to emerge from challenges with increased resilience, wisdom and self-awareness.

**Supportive Networks:** Atheists benefit from supportive networks, both within and outside their community. These networks offer encouragement, resources and a sense of shared experiences.

So atheists approach adversity with a combination of rationality, resilience and reliance on secular principles. They draw on their community, values and personal strategies to navigate challenges, with a focus on problem-solving, ethical living and personal growth. While their worldview may not involve religious beliefs, atheists find strength and meaning in their responses to adversity.

# Chapter 61: Atheist Views on Legacy and Impact

Atheists, like people of any belief system, contemplate their place in the world and the legacy they will leave behind. Despite their disbelief in the supernatural, atheists have meaningful perspectives on how they can make a positive impact during their lifetime and beyond. Let's explore atheist views on legacy, the pursuit of meaning and the desire to leave a lasting impact on the world.

**Secular Legacy:** Atheists view legacy in secular terms, valuing the impact they make on the lives of others and the world through their actions, contributions and values.

**Human-Centered Impact:** Atheists often prioritize making a positive impact on human lives and society. They seek to improve the well-being of individuals and contribute to a more just and equitable world.

**Ethical Living:** Many atheists believe that ethical living is a fundamental part of leaving a positive legacy. They strive to lead principled lives that align with their values, setting an example for others.

**Advocacy and Social Change:** Atheists are often passionate advocates for social change. They engage in activism to address issues like human rights, social justice and secularism, aiming to leave a lasting impact on society.

**Scientific and Intellectual Contributions:** Atheists may emphasize the importance of scientific and intellectual contributions as part of their legacy. They value knowledge and understanding as lasting gifts to humanity.

**Empowering Future Generations:** Atheists see empowering future generations with knowledge, critical thinking skills and ethical values as a way to create a meaningful legacy.

**Personal Relationships:** Atheists understand the significance of personal relationships in their legacy. They aim to nurture positive connections and leave behind memories of love, kindness and support.

**Artistic and Creative Expression:** Atheists often express themselves through art, literature, music and other creative mediums. They view their creative works as a form of legacy, impacting the emotions and thoughts of others.

**Documenting Their Journey:** Some atheists document their life experiences, thoughts and beliefs through writing, blogging, or other forms of storytelling, sharing their insights and perspectives with a wider audience.

**Inspiring Critical Thinking:** Atheists value critical thinking and may seek to inspire it in others. They hope to leave a legacy of independent thought and skepticism toward unfounded claims.

**Environmental Stewardship:** Environmental consciousness is part of the legacy for many atheists. They aim to leave behind a healthier planet for future generations by supporting sustainable practices and conservation efforts.

**Promoting Secular Values:** Atheists often work to promote secular values such as secular government, freedom of thought and separation of church and state, believing that these principles contribute to a more just society.

So atheists approach the idea of legacy with a focus on human-centered impact, ethical living, advocacy and the pursuit of knowledge. While they may not believe in an afterlife, they are motivated to leave a positive and lasting imprint on the world through their actions, contributions and values.

# Chapter 62: The Future of Atheist Spirituality

Atheist spirituality is an evolving and dynamic aspect of contemporary atheism. As the atheist community grows and diversifies, so does the concept of spirituality within this worldview. Let's explore the potential future directions of atheist spirituality and how it may continue to evolve in the years to come.

**Expanding Diversity:** The future of atheist spirituality is likely to witness an even greater diversity of perspectives and practices. As atheists come from various cultural backgrounds, they may incorporate different cultural elements into their spirituality.

**Incorporation of Science:** Given the strong emphasis on reason and science within atheism, the future of atheist spirituality may involve a deeper integration of scientific insights into practices and beliefs, especially regarding the natural world.

**Emerging Rituals and Traditions:** New atheist rituals and traditions may emerge, providing opportunities for atheists to celebrate life events, commemorate milestones and connect with one another in meaningful ways.

**Ethical Frameworks:** The future of atheist spirituality may see the development of more comprehensive ethical frameworks that guide not only individual behavior but also the collective actions of atheist communities.

**Technology and Digital Communities:** With the advancement of technology, atheist communities and spiritual practices may increasingly move into the digital realm. Online forums, virtual gatherings and AI-driven interactions could play a role in shaping the future of atheist spirituality.

**Interfaith Dialogue:** Atheists may continue to engage in interfaith dialogue, promoting understanding and cooperation among individuals with diverse belief systems. These dialogues could contribute to the evolution of atheist spirituality by fostering new perspectives.

**Artistic Expression:** Creative expression through art, music, literature and other mediums may continue to be a prominent aspect of atheist spirituality, providing opportunities for self-expression and connection.

**Environmental Consciousness:** The future of atheist spirituality may involve a stronger emphasis on environmental consciousness and sustainability, as atheists recognize the interconnectedness of humanity with the natural world.

**Social Justice and Activism:** Atheists are likely to remain active in social justice movements, advocating for equal rights, secularism and humanitarian causes. These efforts may be an integral part of their spiritual expression.

**Secular Celebrations:** Atheists may develop secular celebrations that honor the beauty of life, relationships and shared values. These celebrations can provide a sense of community and connection.

**Legacy and Impact:** The future of atheist spirituality may involve a greater focus on the legacy and impact individuals leave behind, emphasizing the importance of living ethically and leaving a positive mark on the world.

So the future of atheist spirituality is likely to be marked by increased diversity, the integration of science and reason, the development of new rituals and traditions and a continued emphasis on ethical living, community and the well-being of both individuals and society. As the atheist community evolves, so too will the ways in which they explore and express their spirituality within a naturalistic worldview.

# Chapter 63: Atheism and the Quest for Knowledge

Atheism is often associated with a commitment to reason, critical thinking and the pursuit of knowledge. While atheism itself is a position on the existence of deities, it also reflects a broader philosophical stance that values evidence-based understanding and seeks to explore the mysteries of the universe. Let's delve into how atheism and the quest for knowledge intersect, highlighting the role of science, skepticism and intellectual curiosity.

**Scientific Inquiry:** Atheists often view science as a powerful tool for understanding the natural world. They appreciate the systematic approach of scientific inquiry, which relies on evidence, observation and empirical investigation.

**Skepticism and Critical Thinking:** Skepticism is a cornerstone of atheism. Atheists value critical thinking and are willing to question beliefs, claims and dogma. They seek rational explanations over supernatural ones.

**Embracing the Unknown:** Atheists are comfortable with the idea that some questions may not have definitive answers. They embrace the unknown and are open to changing their beliefs in light of new evidence.

**Curiosity and Intellectual Exploration:** Atheists are often intellectually curious and value the exploration of a wide range of subjects. They appreciate the pursuit of knowledge as a lifelong journey.

**Reliance on Evidence:** Atheists rely on empirical evidence and logical reasoning when forming their beliefs. They are less likely to accept claims without sufficient support.

**Integration of Knowledge:** Atheists aim to integrate their understanding of the natural world across various disciplines. They seek to synthesize knowledge from science, philosophy, history and other fields.

**Promotion of Education:** Many atheists emphasize the importance of education, both for themselves and for society as a whole. They believe that a well-informed populace is crucial for progress and enlightenment.

**Ethical Considerations:** Atheists often explore the ethical implications of knowledge and scientific advancements. They engage in discussions about responsible use of technology and the potential consequences of human actions.

**Dialogue and Debate:** Atheists value intellectual dialogue and debate. They appreciate the exchange of ideas and the opportunity to refine their understanding through reasoned discussions.

**Humility in the Face of Complexity:** Atheists recognize the complexity of the universe and human understanding. They approach knowledge with humility, understanding that there is always more to learn.

**Inspiration for Progress:** Atheists find inspiration in the pursuit of knowledge. They see science and rational inquiry as tools for addressing societal challenges and improving the human condition.

**Appreciation of Natural Beauty:** The quest for knowledge often leads atheists to a deeper appreciation of the natural world. They marvel at the beauty and intricacy of the universe as revealed by scientific exploration.

So atheism and the quest for knowledge are intertwined in a commitment to rational inquiry, evidence-based understanding and intellectual curiosity. Atheists value science, skepticism and critical thinking as essential tools for exploring the mysteries of the universe and promoting human progress.

# Chapter 64: Conclusion: Embracing a Life of Atheist Spirituality

In this exploration of atheist spirituality, we have journeyed through a worldview that, while disbelieving in the supernatural, is rich with meaning, purpose and connection to the world. Atheist spirituality is a celebration of life, ethics, reason and the human experience. As we conclude our discussion, let's reflect on the key takeaways and the essence of embracing a life of atheist spirituality.

**Atheism and Spirituality:** Atheist spirituality demonstrates that spirituality need not rely on the divine. It can instead center on values, ethics, mindfulness and the awe-inspiring beauty of the natural world.

**Ethical Living:** For atheists, ethical living is a fundamental component of their spirituality. They prioritize empathy, compassion and ethical values in their interactions with others.

**Connection to Nature:** Many atheists find spiritual connection in nature, appreciating its beauty and complexity. Nature serves as a source of inspiration and a reminder of our place in the universe.

**Community and Human Connection:** Building meaningful relationships and engaging in a sense of community are vital aspects of atheist spirituality. These connections provide support, camaraderie and a sense of belonging.

**Intellectual Curiosity:** Atheist spirituality embraces intellectual curiosity and critical thinking. Atheists value the pursuit of knowledge and understanding as a means to navigate life's questions.

**Advocacy and Social Justice:** Atheists often engage in social activism and advocacy for causes they are passionate about, aligning with their commitment to ethical living and social change.

**Legacy and Impact:** Atheists aspire to leave a positive legacy through their actions, contributions and values. They seek to make the world a better place during their lifetime and beyond.

**Embracing the Unknown:** Atheist spirituality encourages an embrace of the unknown and an acceptance that some questions may remain unanswered. It fosters an appreciation for life's mysteries.

**Celebrating Life:** Ultimately, atheist spirituality is a celebration of life itself. It finds meaning, joy and fulfillment in the human experience, relationships and the pursuit of a better world.

So atheist spirituality demonstrates that a life rich in meaning, ethics and connection to the world can flourish without the need for supernatural beliefs. It is a testament to the human capacity for wonder, compassion and personal growth. While it may be distinct from religious spirituality, it offers a unique and valuable path to living a life that is fulfilling, purposeful and deeply connected to the natural world and the diverse tapestry of humanity.

# Epilogue: Reflecting on Our Journey

As we come to the end of this exploration of atheist spirituality, I'm reminded of the rich tapestry of ideas, values and experiences that make up this worldview. While I may have been the voice guiding you through this book, the essence of atheist spirituality lies within the diverse community of individuals who embrace it.

Atheist spirituality is a journey of self-discovery, an ongoing quest for understanding and a celebration of the human experience. It's a worldview that finds wonder in the natural world, meaning in ethical living and purpose in the connections we forge with one another.

In the absence of the divine, atheist spirituality is a testament to our capacity for empathy, compassion and intellectual curiosity. It's a reminder that we are part of a larger whole, connected to the intricate web of life on this planet and the vast cosmos beyond.

As you close this book, I encourage you to carry with you the lessons and insights it has offered. Whether you identify as an atheist or simply seek to better understand the diverse perspectives that shape our world, may you continue to explore, question and celebrate the extraordinary journey of being human.

Remember, atheist spirituality is not a destination but a lifelong exploration. It's a path that encourages us to find beauty in the natural world, seek truth through reason and strive for a more just and compassionate society.

Thank you for joining me on this journey of discovery. May your life be filled with wonder, purpose and the joy of embracing the richness of the human experience.

# About the Author

Tony Churchill is an engaging and thought-provoking author who brings a unique perspective to the world of atheist spirituality. With a background rooted in critical thinking and a passion for exploring the depths of the human experience, Tony offers readers an opportunity to journey into the fascinating realm where atheism and spirituality intersect. As an advocate for reason, ethics, and the celebration of life, Tony invites readers to embrace a worldview that finds wonder in the natural world and meaning in the connections we forge with others. Through insightful exploration and a commitment to open-mindedness, Tony Churchill sparks curiosity and encourages readers to question, learn, and appreciate the diverse tapestry of beliefs that shape our world.